the **WriteStuff!**

POET

MIDLANDS

Edited by Claire Tupholme

First published in Great Britain in 2003 by
YOUNG WRITERS
Remus House,
Coltsfoot Drive,
Peterborough, PE2 9JX
Telephone (01733) 890066

HB ISBN 0 75434 317 0
SB ISBN 0 75434 318 9

FOREWORD

This year, the Young Writers' The Write Stuff! competition proudly presents a showcase of the best poetic talent from over 40,000 up-and-coming writers nationwide.

Young Writers was established in 1991 and we are still successful, even in today's modern world, in promoting and encouraging the reading and writing of poetry.

The thought, effort, imagination and hard work put into each poem impressed us all, and once again, the task of selecting poems was a difficult one, but nevertheless, an enjoyable experience.

We hope you are as pleased as we are with the final selection and that you and your family continue to be entertained with *The Write Stuff! Midlands* for many years to come.

CONTENTS

Kirsty Ford	74
Becky Brown	75
Hollie Goodreid	76
Alex Harnett	76
Daniel Yeo	77
Thomas Stentiford	77
Charlotte Burton	78
Rebecca Buttery	78
Paramveer Gill	79
Lewis Adcock	80
Nadia Bobash	80
Sean Weston	81
Alex Finch	82
Fodoulla Vanezi	82
Daniel Loftus	83
Louise Shenton	84
Charlotte Proud	85
Charlotte Hughes	86
Kellyann Shorter	87
Ian Rowlands	88
Casey Skillen	88
Danny Lindley	89
Hannah Wilcox	90
Joanna Codling	90
Selim Dayanik	91
Henry Goh	92
Philip Bailey	92
Natalie Bayliss	93
Ceri Jones	93
Sarah Vernon	94
Philip Liebman	94
Nicholas Nicholson	95
Ruth Moorhouse	96
Katie Harris	96
Natalie Ball	97
Jenny Pugh	98
Christopher Airey	98
Stewart Murray	99

Hannah Abbiss	99
Bobby Russell	100
Sophie Boden	100
Catherine Rogers	101
Alex Humphries	102
Neil Allard	102
Kim Shepherd	103
Ben Hamilton	104
Kayley Wolfe	104
Tom Pennington	105
Robert Eacock	105
James Hayes	106
Thomas Lewis	107
Leigh Egleton	108
Charlotte Clarke	108
Nicholas Cotterill	109
Sukhdeep Sarai	109
James Whild	110
Amy Eacock	110
Mark Evans	111
Kate Harding-Jack	111
Sam Harrow	112
Abby Clifford	112
Natasha Young	113
Richard Bramall	114
Fiona Jagger	114
Emma Stevens	115
Declan Egerton	116
Carlene Bates	117
Gemma Hedges	118
Ben Hadley-Evans	118
Toni Williams	119
Charlotte Evans	120
Hannah Taylor	120
Stef Badger	121
James Fellows	122
Emily Evans	123
Daniel Bevington	124

The Poems

BRUMMIE LAND

New Street Station,
A large hustling city
Where trains come with a bad stomach pain.
So many rails, you'd think they are becoming extinct
Scrambling up the gradient
And rolling down, with a rumble
And a tumble.

A raging rhino up the tracks,
Its rollerblades going clickety-clack.
A mini city leading away.
The Earth shaking and quivering,
The platforms disappearing.
The wheels are quaking
The birds on the Centenary fly away squawking.

As the hustle and bustle dies down,
We all go into the town for the greatest thing ever -
Birmingham at night.
But it could give you a fright
It is as electrifying as a wire.
The lights are like sparks, rising from a fuse.
Most people here support the blues!
Hear the roar of a dinosaur as Aston Villa score!
We all yell, we want an encore!

It won't be long now, till I'm back in Brum!
Birmingham from morning till night
is everyone's delight!

Daniel Gormley (12)
Bishop Walsh RC School, Sutton Coldfield

IN MY TREE HOUSE

In my tree house, aged seven,
This new place I have encountered is just like Heaven.
My toys and my dolls scattered all over the place,
You can tell I like my new tree house by the curiosity
Written on my face.
I love my tree house so much, I don't want the day to end.
A letter to thank Father Christmas for building it for me, I will send.

In my tree house aged twelve
Into my fantasy world I delve.
New things to do and new things to see
I'm not in my tree house as much as I used to be.
The tree house is the best place to hide
From all the troubles I have outside.
No one can find me there
I just sit there, hugging my bear.
But that's the only time I spend there now,
When my mum and I have had a row.

Looking at the tree house, aged fifteen,
To me, my tree house is a *has-been!*
My tree house is to be pulled down
My smile suddenly turns to a frown.
It means too much to me, no it can't go
Then I see it moving to and fro.
It's gone!
Never to be seen again.
All I can feel is the pain,
I will never forget you - tree house.

Olivia Hines (14)
Bishop Walsh RC School, Sutton Coldfield

ANGEL

Sitting in my room
There're smiles on the outside,
Tears on the in,
My heart and soul in my waste paper bin.

Sitting in my room
Was where I lay
When I first heard the
News on that dismal day.

Sitting in my room
A life came to an end,
Surrounded by gloom
I think, why my friend?

Sitting in my room
I saw a ray of hope,
Just inches before
The noose in my rope.

Sitting in my room
A call from a new love,
Saving me with wings of a dove,
Saving me with holy grace,
She's my favourite face.

Sitting in my room
I'll see an angel out there,
An overcoat is all she'll wear.

Lucas Hadley (14)
Bishop Walsh RC School, Sutton Coldfield

IF I LIVED ON . . .

If I lived on Jupiter, a windy desert land
I would gaze upon the Earth and think that it was small.

If I lived on Pluto, a quiet freezing land
I would look out for the Earth, but see nothing at all.

If I lived on a star, millions of miles away
Would I know about the Earth, the people living there?

If I lived on the sun, hot and very fiery
Would I see the Earth, tiny, floating over there?

I've gone somewhere else now, how I got there's a mystery,
But I have a friend there who is very kind to me.

He dresses in white, his name I do not know,
He has a father, who, he says I should know.

He tells me my father sees and guides you,
My father, he says, is the father of you.

Joe Martin (11)
Bishop Walsh RC School, Sutton Coldfield

FOREVER A STARRY NIGHT

Remember this day forever,
Do not let us fade away,
Over no-man's-land we come together.
'Merry Christmas,' but what else do we say?
Forever a starry night.
What will tomorrow bring?
Though the future is not very bright!

Silent Night is what we sing,
It's a war with no glamour or glory!
For the graves are marked with a wooden stick.
For everyone else there's a different story,
But instead they give us a ball to kick!
Will this war ever cease
Or tomorrow will God bring peace?

Samantha Nugent (17)
Bishop Walsh RC School, Sutton Coldfield

POPPY FIELDS

Strolling along the poppy fields where young men came and died,
I look around the tranquil atmosphere and feel a sense of pride.
As pictures flood my memory and a feeling of guilt sinks in,
I pull out the bottle like the captain did, only half full of gin.

Strolling along the poppy fields where dirt filled men's eyes
A memory of shooting bullets coming at us like flies.
My best friend Bobby was shot in front of me,
Sometimes I was driven to the point of going to flee.

Strolling along the poppy fields where mazes stretch as far
As the eye can see,
Where rain, lice and mud are the only parts of reality,
Where the mist of death nearly hung over me,
Where I would sit and worry about my family.

Strolling along the poppy fields where young men came and died,
I ask myself the question, why did so many have to die?
I wonder if they're angels in Heaven and can fly,
Strolling along in poppy fields where young men came and died.

Charlotte Timmins (14)
Bishop Walsh RC School, Sutton Coldfield

RIDING SKY-HIGH

In the queue I stand and stare
My mind racing, *should I dare?*
We're getting closer whilst my hands shake even more
I don't want to do this, I've never done it before.

My friend turns and looks at me, we're here at last
We're about to get on, my heart beats fast
I sit in the chair, as the bar comes down
I'm getting more worried, I start to frown.

I begin to breathe slowly as we go further up
We're so high, I can't bear to look
Up and down, round and round
Suddenly I look - we're upside down.

The world goes past, people fly by
It feels so good; I'm riding sky-high
It's great, I love it; I scream and shout
What on earth was I worrying about?

In the queue where I stand and stare
No need to worry, I'm without a care.

Catherine Allen (14)
Bishop Walsh RC School, Sutton Coldfield

BIRMINGHAM AT NIGHT

Birmingham at night has the glow of a star!
Noises from the clubs,
Laughing from the city.
The trains rush past
Like low rumbling thunder.

The streets are as crowded as a football ground.
The spire of the Cathedral looks over the city
Like a tall giraffe.
The canals weave in and out of buildings
Like one big, long snake.

Beth Gregory (12)
Bishop Walsh RC School, Sutton Coldfield

BIRMINGHAM CITY FOOTBALL CLUB

Birmingham City, what a pity!
Now let's get down to the nitty-gritty.
They're rubbish,
Steve Bruce's biography will never get published.
The City, a disgrace,
they'll never last the pace.
The boys in blue,
for some reason, they always need the loo.
They're a stupid lot,
they play like tots.
But local rivals must be ashamed,
after the 3-1 victory they proclaimed.
Savage thinks he's pretty.
He-he! Birmingham City.
John's shots are like he's launching a bomb,
when you look up, it's always gone.
Purse's at the back
and he always gets crippled by the attack.
Sisie in the middle,
his ball control is as up and down, like the notes of a fiddle.
Why do they have to represent us?
All they do is embarrass us!

Curtis Clarke (12)
Bishop Walsh RC School, Sutton Coldfield

BIRMINGHAM CITY FC

Steve Bruce is the best,
Brought Birmingham to the rest,
Stern John, Cisse, Horsfield too,
Savage with his hair not new,
We'll try our best to stay up,
We will win the Premiership Cup,
Aston Villa, not a thriller,
West Brom, are not a killer,
3-0 at Villa Park,
Enkleman what a lark,
We are Birmingham City.

We overcame the power of Leeds,
It was like swimming through reeds,
They thought we'd lose facing the cop,
Clinton Morisson had a pop,
In the goal, across the line,
That was it for extra time,
We'll play our best,
Although Villa are a pest,
Keep right on to the end.

Ben Gould (12)
Bishop Walsh RC School, Sutton Coldfield

STUCK IN THE JAM

In the car off on our holidays,
We drive and drive down the motorways.
We set out our route to Amsterdam,
Then, oh no, we're stuck in the jam.

Cars beep their horns as anger sets in,
Shut up will you, pack it in.
I eat my sandwich filled with ham,
Here we are still stuck in the jam.

It's been so long, are we nearly there?
It's getting too hot, it's too hard to bear.
I'm getting so bored with Uncle Peter and Auntie Pam,
Are we ever going to get out of being stuck in the jam?

Nichola Tohill (14)
Bishop Walsh RC School, Sutton Coldfield

BONFIRE NIGHT

Crack, bang, hiss,
As fireworks shoot in the sky.
Bursts of colour and light,
Sparkle, flash, dazzle!

Children scream, spines tingle,
Ears ring in the silence.
The Catherine wheel sizzles, then fizzles out
And the final bang dies away.

Flames dance in the moonlight,
Hissing, leaping, licking!
Sparks crackle and spit
As the scorching fire blazes.

All this because of one man
Who hatched an evil plan,
To kill King James I
And blow up the Houses of Parliament.

But his dastardly plot was crushed
When he was arrested on November 4th.
He was tortured and burnt at the stake
And is remembered on Bonfire Night!

Emma Gould (12)
Bishop Walsh RC School, Sutton Coldfield

IMAGES IN THE SKY

I went out one day
because I wanted to play.

First outside comes my mother,
second my brother.

Then my mum gave a shout
and I found out

that from the sky
don't ask me why,

there came a ship
making a trip.

Then I shouted out loud,
'Oh, it's only a cloud.'

Mum, go and get your glasses
before it passes.

Thomas Gallagher (11)
Bishop Walsh RC School, Sutton Coldfield

SUMMER HOLIDAYS

On Blackpool beach having fun,
Sitting out in the warm sun,
We all sit eating ice cream,
Tanning in the hot beam.

Little children making sandcastles,
Grown-ups forgetting all their hassles,
No one worrying about a thing,
Thinking what the holiday will bring.

Splashing around in the sea,
Happy as I could ever be,
Thinking of postcards I'll have to send,
Never wanting this to end.

Anna Sweeting (14)
Bishop Walsh RC School, Sutton Coldfield

SLAVE'S FREEDOM

On the northern railroad, where I drink till I fall,
The squeaky track just winds on,
It drives me up the wall,
Slaves all sing. Sorrowful,
I cower away and hide,
I was one of them till I ran away,
My heart had already died.

On the northern railroad, the hobos pass us by,
They tell of hidden lands
Where man dare not fly.

On the northern railroad, my life scars will pass,
But I fear my brain says, *'Stop!*
Just fill me another glass.'

On the northern railroad, I give up and say,
'One way ticket for me sir.'
Don't disturb, let me lay.

On the northern railroad, my life drifts away,
It's all over now,
There's nothing left to say.

Aaron McKenna (14)
Bishop Walsh RC School, Sutton Coldfield

BIRMINGHAM'S BEAUTIFUL CANALS

The Brummie's canals
    Are beautiful things.
        They wiggle like worms
    Everywhere,
  They are a continual
Swarm of angry bees
  Not knowing
    Where they are going.
        The reflection of the light
    Shimmers like stars on a
  Blanket of dark blue,
The boats are the
  Gods of the waterways,
    Gracefully travelling, where
        They want to go.

Connor Ruffinato (12)
Bishop Walsh RC School, Sutton Coldfield

SPAGHETTI JUNCTION

Lots of spaghetti, piled up on a plate,
Boring and dull, the humming of the cars
As they go round and round,
In different directions.
One after the other,
Day by day,
The same routine.

Lucy Shaw (12)
Bishop Walsh RC School, Sutton Coldfield

CHORES

In the hospital and I'm feeling fine,
(Don't know what all the fuss is about),
My mum says she would wait, but hadn't the time,
My family are leaving and I'm filling up,
'Are you OK?' the nurse says to me.
I reply, 'Yeah, I s'pose, as well as can be.'

In the hospital and I'm feeling sick,
'Can I have some help please?'
'Yes of course, I won't be a tick.'
I listen to God and fall to my knees,
Oh please help me God. Please.

In the hospital and I'm feeling better,
The rain outside, I'm getting wetter and wetter,
I arrive at my house door,
My mum says, 'We're glad to have you back,
But get on with your chores!'

Michael Colledge (14)
Bishop Walsh RC School, Sutton Coldfield

BIRMINGHAM AT NIGHT

Birmingham is still, day at night,
The noise is like the cheer of the crowd, when a goal is scored.
The traffic is like a giant's thunderous footsteps.
The music is as loud as a stampede of elephants and rhinos.
The sites are as alive as you and I are, as beautiful
As the setting of the sun.
The lights are as bright as the sun and
The night sky is as mysteriously dark as the underworld.
The excitement is as exhilarating as a roller coaster.
For Birmingham is the city that never sleeps.

Christopher Vas (12)
Bishop Walsh RC School, Sutton Coldfield

EARTH TREMOR, EARTH TERROR

The tremor, like a giant crane machine
lifting a blue whale and dropping it down,
letting it rapidly fall onto the hard, rough ground.

The sound, like a giant ship moaning
as it sinks deep into the crystal ocean,
emerged with the noise of a giant's stomach rumbling.

Scared with fright, people are still, like ice.
Terrified that they will fall into the core of the Earth.

The thought of goblins reaching up through the ground,
grasping me and pulling me down,
out of my world, is disturbing.

I open my eyes, I am still here,
no movement in sight.
I have no fear, the tremor
has passed away.

Lauren Canavan (12)
Bishop Walsh RC School, Sutton Coldfield

BIRMINGHAM IN THE NIGHT SKY

The bright lights shine like the sun
People pour onto the streets, like a swarm of bees.
The *boom, boom, boom* of the clubs,
The roar of the roller coaster is heard for miles around.
Exciting is a good night out,
The drink, people confused.
The black of the starry night sky.

Ian Hoverd (13)
Bishop Walsh RC School, Sutton Coldfield

First In To Bat!

Walking up to the stumps,
First in to bat,
Waiting for the umpire to say play,
The bowler runs up, that was flat.

Waiting for it to arrive,
Running up to the spot,
I thought this is a good ball,
That was hot.

Ninety miles an hour, coming at speed,
Swinging in, swinging out,
Reading the ball like never before,
Thinking to myself, that ball was against the law.

Sixth ball round, waiting and waiting,
Always waiting to play that mysterious shot,
Wishing you won't hear that sound,
The bowler comes up and frowns.

Helen Shipman (11)
Bishop Walsh RC School, Sutton Coldfield

Spaghetti Junction

A nest full of paths.

Ants marching around
Driving in rhythm
With a deafening sound!
Colours and *shapes*
Lighting up the dark
Fight!
Through the traffic
there's no time to lark!

Lauren Hill (13)
Bishop Walsh RC School, Sutton Coldfield

FIRE

The flames begin to grow,
With every second that passes the fire doubles,
Burning anything in its path.
Getting bigger and bigger
Until the house that started the fire is too small,
So the deadly flames smash through the windows
And burst open the doors.

Until the fire followed its forest victim,
Firing flaming bullets,
Crisping the trees, ready to devour.
The fire marched to the bush,
Without warning
Went in for the kill.
Fattening on its prey,
Growing angrier, ramming everything out the way.

Not even man could stop him!

Elliot Geddes (11)
Bishop Walsh RC School, Sutton Coldfield

BREAK

Down in the lockers, surrounded by a crowd,
Everybody shouting and laughing out loud.
The rain drumming down furiously outside
Whilst we eat, chat and have a good time.

Down in the lockers, catching up on work
Everyone's excited and going berserk.
Glad to get away from the boring lessons
All the listening, writing and ridiculous questions!

Down in the lockers, having loads of fun
Everyone thinks the work is all done.
But at half-past eleven, I hear the sound of the bell
It's so unfair, we have to go back to this hell!

Natalie Flood (15)
Bishop Walsh RC School, Sutton Coldfield

IT'S WINTER

Snowflakes falling,
It's winter.
Icicles resting on windows,
It's winter.
Children playing,
It's winter.
Woolly hats, gloves and scarves,
It's winter.
Building snowmen,
It's winter.
Snowball fights,
It's winter.
Sledging down hills,
It's winter.
Wet clothes and wellies,
It's winter.
Little red noses,
It's winter.
Bright warm fires,
It's winter.
Hot mug of cocoa,
It's winter.

Katie Lee (12)
Bishop Walsh RC School, Sutton Coldfield

THE TEST

In the exam hall, racking my brains,
I look outside, it's driving rain.
I look all around me, then look to the floor,
I guess I should have revised more.

In the exam hall, everyone near me is writing so fast,
I cannot believe it. I am never going to pass!
I glance up for some inspiration,
Then back down in desperation.

In the exam hall, I turn the page. Hoping to see,
Oh yes, this cannot be!
I know this topic and all its facts,
I push my knowledge to the max.

Maybe I will make the grade,
Pass maths and you're made!
I smile to myself,
Then turn the page . . .

Siobhan Woulfe (14)
Bishop Walsh RC School, Sutton Coldfield

FOUR STEPS BEHIND

In the park where we both stood
Dark and mysterious, we really should.
One step closer, my feet on the floor
We're nearly there now, just a little bit more.

Running through the streets, no looking back.
Hurry . . . come on or he'll give us a whack.
One step closer, my feet on the floor
We're nearly there now, just a little bit more.

We're here now, where we want to be.
The only problem is, we cannot see.
One step back, my feet in the air,
He's gone from here, did he *really* care?

Sinéad Chantel Maher (14)
Bishop Walsh RC School, Sutton Coldfield

VICTORIOUS GUNNERS

The top guns run out onto the green turf,
The crowd roar for their heroes,
Small boys and big men sit at home glued to the television,
The match has begun.

The coin is flicked and Arsenal choose,
The crowd roar for their heroes.
Kick-off - the tension rises in the stand and on the pitch,
The time starts ticking away.

The first goal is scored by United,
The crowd roar for their heroes.
The Gunners need a goal, they press the opposition,
Half-time has arrived.

Vieira leads the champions onto the pitch,
The crowd roar for their heroes.
Freddie Ljunberg gets the equaliser,
There is still time to win.

The Highbury boys keep fighting,
The crowd roar for their heroes.
Henry scores two in the ninetieth minute,
Full-time arrives,
Now the crowd *seriously* roar for their proven heroes.

Luke Perry (11)
Bishop Walsh RC School, Sutton Coldfield

A Day In The Life Of . . .
Birmingham New Street Station

Birmingham New Street Station, busy as ever
You couldn't even hear a ten ton boulder fall.
The hustle and bustle of workers going to work;
Like a herd of elephants off stomping.
The red of frustration is showing.
Hurry up! Get out of my way!

But once everyone has gone,
It is as quiet as a mouse.
But soon rush hour will be back, as busy as ever.
But now, everyone is purple with relaxation.
But once they're all at home again -
It is as deserted as a desert.

This is a day in the life of . . .
Birmingham New Street Station.

Thomas Astell (12)
Bishop Walsh RC School, Sutton Coldfield

Anger

Anger is red,
The taste of poison in your blood
And the smell of blinding smoke.
It looks like lightning
And sounds like thunder.
Anger feels like a cage
And you can't break free.

Joseph Killian (11)
Bishop Walsh RC School, Sutton Coldfield

VILLA PARK

Villa Park is a hooligan magnet
It is a bright or dark colour
Depending on the score.
It is a lion
Screaming its loudest roar.
It is tense
Everyone in suspense,
Then as suddenly
As a tiger pouncing on a deer
Everything is lost.
The losers are in fear.

This is football
At its best!

Aston Villa FC.

William Capper (13)
Bishop Walsh RC School, Sutton Coldfield

ANGER

Anger is a terrible thing,
It lurks inside each of us
Waiting to show its ugly face,
To wreak havoc in our lives.
It sends us to an early grave,
So bury your anger not your body.
Control your fists,
Control your mind,
Find a smile
And share it with us.

David Haynes (11)
Bishop Walsh RC School, Sutton Coldfield

THE ONE DAY TRUCE

The spirit of peace reached even us here,
Out on the trench, away from our loved ones.
A simple game of football made the enemies near
To our hearts and with the songs
We sang together like old chums.
That day history was made.
'I wish every day,' said Bruce,
'Could be like the one day truce.'

We played and sang until midnight,
We went to bed as both sides united as one.
The next day we had to resume the fight.
The world would not forget what we had done.
'I wish every day,' said Bruce,
'Could be like the one day truce.'

Fay Sutton (17)
Bishop Walsh RC School, Sutton Coldfield

CANAL

A twisted snake,
A knotted rope.
The continuing path
It moves like the moon, round and round
Being churned in God's mouth . . .
The water skids down its man-made track,
Then the weight of a boat pushes . . .
So it pushes back.
A muddy eruption
The colour as changeable as a TV
Brown as chocolate
White froth flows, like the top of a beer.

Kieran Flynn (12)
Bishop Walsh RC School, Sutton Coldfield

SCHOOLS

Oh no, it's Monday morning,
It's time for school again.
The day is nearly dawning,
It's driving me insane.

The weekend, it has gone so fast,
I didn't see it pass.
Now it's time to get my books
And get back into class.

It's French at nine to start the day,
All this fancy chat.
I can't remember anything,
What is French for rat?

Break time's next, gotta dash,
Gotta grab a snack.
Just ten minutes to have some fun,
Then we will be back.

It's lunchtime now, we must all rush
To be first in the queue.
Chips, pizza and snacks galore,
Honestly, it's true.

End of school is coming,
Bell's about to ring.
Silence absorbs the crowd
As the bell goes *bring, bring.*

Sophie Patterson (11)
Bishop Walsh RC School, Sutton Coldfield

NOWHERE

In the middle of nowhere
I lie all alone
Wishing I have credit on my mobile phone.
People are mean and don't care about me,
I'll get out of here, just wait and see.

In the middle of nowhere
Lying here in my bed,
With a big white bandage wrapped around my head.
It wasn't his fault, I don't blame him,
But he *did* drink too much gin.

In the middle of nowhere
The nurse leaves the room,
I remember what happened and I know that I'm doomed.
Why didn't I get a chance? So many things unsaid,
But the car's all smashed up and my dad is dead.

Lara Hayes (14)
Bishop Walsh RC School, Sutton Coldfield

UP AT THE WINDOW . . .

Up at the window I could hear birds sing
And the thoughts in my head were like bells that would ring.
I tried to let go but still they were there,
Those thoughts in my head really could scare.

Up at the window the voices would say:
'Just let go, don't go on like this every day.'
I tried to tell myself it couldn't be true,
But it all started the day I fell in love with you.

Up at the window now I'm with you,
I'm glad I followed my heart, which was true.
We can spend our lives together,
I hope we stay in love forever.

Lucy Cunningham (15)
Bishop Walsh RC School, Sutton Coldfield

The Drawer Of Mystery

Creeping, creeping up the stairs
To see what the secret drawer will bear.
Gold, diamonds or rubies maybe?
We will have to wait and see.

I tiptoe into the room with care,
If Mom was to see me she'd go spare.
Now to the dresser I must go,
To open the drawer I crouch down low.

Oh no! What's that noise I hear?
Someone must be coming near.
I quickly slither under the bed,
Better make sure I don't bang my head.

Mom enters the room singing loudly,
As she opens *the* drawer she smiles proudly.
I lean forward; then stop and stare,
There's my first tooth and lock of hair.

The things in the drawer,
Mom looks at in wonder and awe.
These blissful memories are her treasures,
Her love for me is beyond measure!

Anna McDonagh (12)
Bishop Walsh RC School, Sutton Coldfield

A Day To Be Proud Of

Men from either side came out,
Met on neutral ground.
Each took turns to shout
And wave back without a sound.
The enemies moved nearer and nearer,
Until close enough to touch,
Soon the objective became clearer,
That none were there to watch.
Gifts and presents were now swapped
Between the two great foes.
For on that day both had stopped
The bloody battle of woe.
Then that day became but a trace,
A twinkling smile on a soldier's face.

Lucy Halliday (17)
Bishop Walsh RC School, Sutton Coldfield

New Street

The stampede of rushing rhinos
Squeezed into one place
Like a rumbling stomach
As the trains pull into the station.
The angry call
Of the Earth,
Trying to get through the mayhem.
Rushing zebras
Escaping
From the danger which lies ahead.
The colour red emerges
All around, as the frustration
Increases on people's faces.

Claire Kelly (12)
Bishop Walsh RC School, Sutton Coldfield

CANALS

Peaceful
      waters
            flowing softly,
               children
            wave as
      boats
   go by.
Parents
      hold on
          tightly
               to them
          underneath
        a
      sunny
   sky.
'Don't fall in!'
      they tell
          their children.
              'Stay away from
                 the waterside.'
             Boats
         drift by
      like little
   ducklings,
      through shining
         water they
           swiftly
               glide.

Helen Kinsella (12)
Bishop Walsh RC School, Sutton Coldfield

MONDAY TO FRIDAY

Every lesson always the same,
The register's read, 'Yes sir,' at my name.
He starts to speak, what a bore,
I'm going to scream, can't take any more.

Every lesson always the same,
Get out my book, 'What's the title again?'
I begin to write, I start off slow.
I get an idea and away I go.

Every lesson always the same,
Finished the question, completed the aim.
The bell rings, I leave and I'm gone,
Down the corridor to my next lesson.

Claire Robinson (14)
Bishop Walsh RC School, Sutton Coldfield

CHRISTMAS DAY

Listen now, the truth will be told;
We did not hate each other, the
Revelation will unfold. Gifts of
Grace, there were gifts of peace; the
Fighting, the death, did at last upon
This day, cease! Mutual harmony and
'One' common aim, for our desires
Were, surprisingly, the same.

'These are the enemies,' so we've been
Told, 'Kill those blasted Germans!'
But who'll pray for us when we're cold?
Beneath the ground we are forgotten, for
Our purpose has gone and our rivalry
Forever rotten!

Sarah Hayes (17)
Bishop Walsh RC School, Sutton Coldfield

ON THE PLAYGROUND

On the playground where the bully stands tall
where he feels big and I feel small.
When he grabs my coat and throws me down
in my emotions and tears I will drown.

'Just ignore him, he's a selfish fool,'
but I know he'll get me outside of school.
All the days I've moaned, cried and wept
all the nights filled with nightmares, where I have not slept.

But now I feel big and free from worry
whilst he must weep away, in Surrey.
For he went too far and stole some cars
and now he feels small, all alone, behind bars.

James Capper (14)
Bishop Walsh RC School, Sutton Coldfield

ODE TO THE BUTCHERS

As the tripe whizzed past my ears
And the chicken pecked my cheek.
The honeyed ham, she sat me down,
While my good friend Veal spoke to the window man.

As the cod whizzed past my ears
And the trollop told a tale.
Good King Salmon offered me a drink
While the wizened crab peeled spuds in the sink.

As the tears rolled past my eyes
And I kissed my friends goodbye.
I turned to face a hellish world,
While vegetables snort and sneer, I just sigh.

But I am better than them, just let them wait and see.

Paul Fleming (14)
Bishop Walsh RC School, Sutton Coldfield

THE NEW BOY!

He came in the doors, sheepish and shy,
Hmmm, I wondered who is this guy?
Whispers of 'new boy' went round the class,
Teacher said, 'Everyone this is Joe Marsh.
His parents have moved here from the US of A,
I hope you'll make him feel very welcome today.'
Joe was sent to a seat right next to me,
He sat down and started to chuckle, 'Hee, hee,
I think our teacher has got things a big wrong,
You can tell by my accent that I'm from Hong Kong.'

Louis Yates
Bishop Walsh RC School, Sutton Coldfield

ON THE TRAIN

Sitting on the train with nothing to do
I'll look out the window and watch the cows go moo!
The cows got too boring, so I looked at the sheep,
Struggling to get over the gate, with a leap.

Looking round the cabin, all I do is stare,
Oh my god, look that man's got really bad hair!
I can't stare any more, it's known to be rude,
If I was him and he was me, I'd feel a bit crude.

I rest my head and try and get some sleep,
Suddenly my phone starts to beep.
It was my boss, I had lots of work but how?
I had something to do and it had to be done *now!*

Olivia Byrne (14)
Bishop Walsh RC School, Sutton Coldfield

THE MEAL

I look on expectantly as the starter rolls in,
She's looking back at me over the gin,
I stare back, a smile upon my face,
She moves her hands upon mine with amazing grace.

I look on expectantly as the main course rolls in,
She is staring at me, on her face, a grin,
I move my chair closer, so does she,
She moves herself closer, closer to me.

I look on expectantly as the dessert rolls in,
Her dress is black and silky, her gold necklace is thin,
The both of us lean over, the flambé gives a hiss,
Then the moment's here, on my lips, a kiss!

Adam Lines (14)
Bishop Walsh RC School, Sutton Coldfield

My Twin Brothers

In form and feature, face and limb,
I grew so like my brother
That folks kept taking me for him
And each for one another.
It puzzled both him and me,
It reached a fearful pitch
For one of us was born a twin,
Yet not a soul knew which.

One day, before our names were fixed
As we were being washed by nurse,
We got completely mixed
And there you see by fate's decree,
(Or rather nurse's whim)
My brother John got christened me
And I got christened him.

The fatal likeness even dogged
My footsteps when at school
And I was always getting flogged
For John turned out a fool,
I put this question hopefully
To everyone I knew -
What would you do, if you were I, to prove that you were you?

Our close resemblance turned the tide
Of my so hard life,
For somehow my intended bride
Became my brother's wife,
Short year after year
Absurd mistakes went on
And when I died the neighbours came
And buried brother John.

Lian Stephenson (11)
Bishop Walsh RC School, Sutton Coldfield

AROUND THE WORLD

First we go to the USA
Over the Lake Ontario.
Also the state of Texas
And now for a break in Colorado

Now we go into the jungle
At the height of the river below
And now on to the tall Andes
Let's fly past Montevideo

Let's stop home in London
Take a look at Bosnia
Then visit Slovenia
And let's stop at Romania

Let's peer at Kazakhstan
Turn around to Turkmenistan
Marvel at Uzbekistan
And finally, Pakistan

Look! There's Algeria
And there's Tunisia
Cool! There's Nigeria
Lastly, there's Libya

Can we go to Australia?
We'll be back in Caledonia
Then we'll swim over the Coral Sea
And finish in Tasmania

Finally Antarctica
Let's walk by Asuka
Let's stop at the South Pole
And now we're done . . . *Eureka!*

James Dickenson (12)
Bishop Walsh RC School, Sutton Coldfield

THE CROWD HAVE SPOKEN

'Let him hang,' the crowd roared,
Suddenly my heart rate soared,
So many people hated me,
If they could only see.

'Let him hang,' the crowd hollered,
That fear of death only followed.
'I didn't do it,' I blurted,
But the court had been sculptured.

'Let him hang,' the crowd pleaded,
As I walked upon the platform,
Let him die,
Let him die.

Edward Gudgeon (14)
Bishop Walsh RC School, Sutton Coldfield

MATCH DAY

At St Andrew's on match day,
The bad weather always stays away,
The pitch green as ever,
We never lose at home, never.

At St Andrew's the ground has started to fill,
You could just tell we will beat the Villa three-nil,
The crowd begin to roar,
As Morrison is about to score.

At St Andrew's we all begin to cheer,
We can all tell that Enkleman is on the beer,
But as Horsfield scored our third goal,
I knew we had ripped out Villa's soul.

Matthew Embrey (14)
Bishop Walsh RC School, Sutton Coldfield

THE DOG WITH A PINK NOSE

She looks up at me with hazel eyes,
'Go away,' my mother cries.
She jumps down, forbidden to be fed
And slinks off back to her own bed.
She now follows me wherever I go,
Says, 'I'm just the dog with the pink nose.'

She looks up at me with pleading eyes
As if to say, 'That cushion's my size.'
She sits and waits so patiently,
Just watching for that nod from me.
She leaps up and drops into a doze,
Says, 'I'm just the dog with the pink nose.'

She looks up at me with mischievous eyes,
She rolls in mud and attracts the flies.
We can't let her in, but she tries to resist,
She gallops right in, not getting the gist.
I attempt to soak her using the hose,
Says, 'I'm just the dog with the pink nose.'

She looks up at me with excited eyes,
'Take me now for some exercise!'
She races to the door, her tail going mad
Indicating that she's happy, not sad.
She's still as a hunter, leaping on her toes,
'Now, I'm the dog with the black nose!'

Kirsten Kimmet (12)
Bishop Walsh RC School, Sutton Coldfield

NEW STREET STATION

As fast as a cheetah
The roar of a lion
The screech of a tyre
The talking of people on their mobile phones
As they go
        to
           different
               platforms.
The shouts of commotion
The
    stairs
        are
          jam-packed
The purpleness of faces
As they are about to *explode.*

Adele Adeniran (12)
Bishop Walsh RC School, Sutton Coldfield

EARTH TREMOR

The earth tremor is about to start,
Nothing can stop it.
The dogs are growling, anxious to get away,
The Earth is going to part,
Nobody knows what they're going to do.
The ground is shaking violently,
What is happening?
There is something under our feet,
The atmosphere is exhilarating and there is no way out.

The sound is like a train coming into New Street,
It came and went like a bouncy ball.
The power was unimaginable and could rip everything apart.
The Earth has gone silent once again,
It has gone back to its underground burrow
And it will return another day.

Matthew Foulds (12)
Bishop Walsh RC School, Sutton Coldfield

IN MY MIND . . .

In my mind I think about,
How you speak and how you shout.
I try to ignore how I feel inside
And all the many times I have lied.

In my mind I think about,
Whether you are too in doubt.
Why I feel the way I do,
It's really strange, it's just brand new.
I don't know how to cure this pain,
For watching you is making me sane.

In my mind I think about
How to blot this feeling out,
But the fact is that I never will,
My love for you makes me feel ill.

Katie Parrish (14)
Bishop Walsh RC School, Sutton Coldfield

THE GREAT OAK

He stands so tall, he stands so proud
As the traffic makes him choke,
For him the car horns are devastatingly loud
And he has to inhale their smoke.

In him we place our trust as we lean on his mighty bulk
And find out from our learned chums how tall we shall grow.
He isn't one to cry and certainly wouldn't sulk.
What emotion does he feel, as he looks on us so low?

They want to cut him down you see,
The mighty oak will live no longer,
In his place four houses will be,
We shan't forget, don't worry, our love is so much stronger.

Martin Woolf (14)
Bishop Walsh RC School, Sutton Coldfield

BIRMINGHAM AT NIGHT

A sleek, furry, black leopard
a hyperactive puppy!
The gentle slumber of his rest
the snappy yaps of a lonely mind

Calm like a lake of crystals
energetic like a sparkling ruby
Tempting you to relax tonight
tempting you to paint the town!

As much sensitivity as a forbidden beach
as many bright lights as the theatre stage . . .

Rosaleen Gallagher (12)
Bishop Walsh RC School, Sutton Coldfield

A HERO'S DEATH

A hero's death was his, Miss Hill,
Fighting in the trenches, a thirst for a kill.
His time had come, he'd done his best
Until a bullet smashed his chest.

A hero's death was his, Miss Hill,
Of this platoon a member still.
He fought with passion, he fought with pride,
Never has such a great fighter died.

A hero's death wasn't his, Miss Hill,
Right down my spine I feel a chill.
He didn't want a blindfold, he wanted to see
The men all bent down on a single knee.

Arms cocked, guns ready, waiting for a final call.
Bullet after bullet your sweetheart fell to the floor.
His eyes were wide open, he called out your name,
Execution for such a good man is an awful shame.

We murder a soldier and cover his death -
The Kaiser couldn't have made a better mess.
His body just lay there, bloody and dead
Covered in holes and full of British lead.

A hero's death wasn't his, Miss Hill,
Across the floor we saw his innocent blood spill.
I see your tears and wonder why?
Why did this deserter have to die?

Fear sentenced your sweetheart, Miss Hill,
But the British Army's pride carried out the kill.
We all walk away, no one need ever know,
We'll continue this masquerade, this British Army show.

Helen Carey (14)
Bishop Walsh RC School, Sutton Coldfield

MY FAMILY

We are a family of four,
Oh . . . what a bore!
There's me and my brother,
My mum and my dad,
Oh . . . and the hamster
But definitely no other!

Sometimes we stay in,
Sometimes we go out
But nowhere exciting,
It's either here or about!
Except (I forgot) . . .
The times I went . . .

To a scary movie,
Holidays far away,
Abseiled down a wall
(And climbed back up a rock face - groovy),
Racing in a sand yacht,
Wow! that's quite a lot.
In fact (I nearly forgot) . . .

My family of four
(And the hamster
From Leicester)
Are not really a bore!
There I go again, we are a bore
When . . .

We don't go out on a Saturday
And I have to do my homework on Sunday,
Then hand it in on a Monday!

Helen Saul (11)
Bishop Walsh RC School, Sutton Coldfield

THE CIRCUS

Hello and welcome to Jim Bob's circus,
What are you here to see?
Is it kangaroos, wombats and bees
Or is it the clowns with their knobbly knees?

So come on, relax and talk to me,
Tell me what you want to see,
I bet you'll want to see the trapeze
Performed by Kelly and Eloise,
Flying high in the sky
Flies Eloise.

The tigers obey
Their Ringmaster's command,
As he cracks his whip
They turn around
And lie down till their next command.

What's this I hear?
The juggling clowns
Giggling and laughing they twirl around,
5, 6, 7, 8 balls all at once,
This must be a record all at once.

Here comes the ponies,
Glistening white,
The clowns on their backs look ready to fight,
The crack of the whip
Makes them run,
Circling the Ringmaster is their kind of fun!

So now it's late
And past time for bed,
Goodnight and farewell
From everyone here at Jim Bob's Circus!

Laura Dudley (11)
Bishop Walsh RC School, Sutton Coldfield

I'M IN LOVE WITH YOU

Tears in my eyes,
Pain in my heart,
I'll never be happy
Whilst we are apart.

No letter that I write to you
Says half the things I want them to,
For how can words reveal a part
Of all the feelings in my heart?
A prayer, a kiss, a smile, a touch
Proves I love you oh so much.

I'm always thinking of you,
Longing to hold you tight.
I'm always dreaming of you
Through each long, lonely night.
I do truly love you
In a very special way
And I'll show you just how much
When I'm at home to stay.

I will give up half my life,
Give up my love life too
Now I have a special girl
As wonderful as you.

In my heart you'll stay forever
Until my heart is through,
So until then darling, remember
I'll forever be in love with you.

Tears in my eyes,
Pain in my heart,
I'll never be happy
Whilst we are apart.

Gareth Richardson (14)
Langley High School, Oldbury

THE DAY I LET YOU GO

Tears on my pillow,
Pain in my heart,
The day I had to leave you
My world fell apart.

No one knows the heartache
I've tried so hard to hide.
No one knows how many times
I've broken down and cried.

Life is grey without you,
The days, they go so slow,
But in my heart you'll always be
Because I love you so.

This sadness I am feeling
Each day that I am away,
The things I have done,
The time I have to pay.

I lie and wonder why it is
I do these foolish things
And what pleasure do I get
And lonely days it brings.

Please try to understand me
That all I need is you.
A place to settle down in,
In warmth and comfort too.

I know we are not side-by-side,
I know we are apart
But no matter where you go
You'll always have my heart,
But please remember most of all
I'll always love you true.

Sajad Ashraf (14)
Langley High School, Oldbury

THE SEASONS

The wind is racing in the sky,
Across the snow and mountains high,
Look out the window and see
All the wonders that can be.

The snow is sliding down
Like a slide I wonder how,
Little snowflakes like a bird
And the race carts that you heard.

The rain is dripping down,
Out of each other,
Rainclouds disappear,
Then the bee flies near.

Spring is near, flowers appear,
Then there're a few deer,
Babies cry, then mothers sigh,
Then all is silent.

Lois Wilkinson (12)
Perryfields High School, Oldbury

NOW YOU'RE GONE

Oh no, what shall I do?
Now you're gone I'm always blue.
You were the one who filled my days
With happiness in lots of ways.

I miss you so much, I hope you're well,
I miss you in a way I cannot tell.
The way you joked with me, the way you provoked me,
The way you played me, the way you made me.

Losing you was very hard,
I never really said goodbye,
So here's my poem just for you,
To ask you *why, why, why?*

Why you?

Amy Neale (15)
Perryfields High School, Oldbury

WHAT AM I?

What am I?
I become, then die, then become again,
In lots of different things,
In plants, in mammals, in reptiles,
In a hummingbird that sings!

What am I?
I stay for long and sometimes short,
I can be happy and depressed,
I go through many stages,
From OK, to worse, to best.

What am I?
I'm new and fresh at springtime,
When old, I'm wise at heart,
I've made all the world just come alive,
You know - I'm pretty smart!

So have you figured me out yet?
You really can't go wrong,
I end in 'e' and begin with 'l',
Come on, I'm not that long!

The word that you are looking for exists in everyone,
You may choose to be in peace, or you may choose to be in strife,
Whichever you decide - the word I am is *life!*

Sascha Williams (13)
Perryfields High School, Oldbury

REALITY OF LOVE

I looked at the way they acted together
And thought that's how I'd like to be,
They used to hug and kiss each other,
I hated it in front of me.

But now it has started to differ,
The love only works from one part.
I look upon them longingly,
How did they grow apart?

Sometimes they are at each other's throats
More often than not.
It's how I wish to see them kiss
To prove the love deep in their hearts.

I look at love with naivety,
It's not always smiles and kisses.
A good job my parents have done to show
Love is different to your wishes.

Sarah Rowlands (15)
Perryfields High School, Oldbury

ALONE

A vagrant's life is full of fears,
Full of hunger, blood spilt and tears.
A life of begging and buying tea,
Is this the life for me?

Walking around every day
Watching everyone else's life pass away.
Wondering when I'll be safe again,
Away from the cold and the rain.

Trying to find a corner to sleep,
Somewhere to live, somewhere to keep,
But the next day it will be gone,
In comes the rain, out goes the sun.

Now I'm cold, wet and sad,
Is homeless life really this bad?
But I know someday I'll see
How really bad homeless life can be.

Kathleen Bone (15)
Perryfields High School, Oldbury

WOMEN ARE . . .

Women are caring,
Women are loving,
Women have babies for demanding hubbies,
Women are fairer,
Women are clever,
Women have problems like hurtful tummies etc,
Women are independent,
Women aren't shy,
Women have bodies that make them cry,
Women are special,
Women are good,
Women can drink more than they think they could,
Women are girly,
Women are (mentally) strong,
Women love buying a really nice thong,
Women are careful with all that they do
And women remember exactly with who!

Nicola Lacey (16)
Perryfields High School, Oldbury

WHAT ARE POEMS?

W hen I was little I asked what were poems?
H ow did people think of such strange words
A nd why did they want to write them to start off with?
T houghts were making me think why are poems exciting?

A re they really worth all that fuss?
R hyming and making them shorter or longer is just a waste of time!
E veryone says that poems aren't read, or are they?

P eople don't realise how much work goes into a poem!
O ften people say that poems are great without even reading them!
E ven some teachers don't know what poems are!
M any people say that you can't beat a good poem!
S o what are poems?

Kate Snaddon (12)
Perryfields High School, Oldbury

BLACK

Deep in thought, drifting in space,
A mystery to the human race.

Evil reigns, such secret plans,
No one knows what's in the future's hands.
Infinity through my mind,
Dark forces rising, stopping time.
Senseless wars, people dead,
Armageddon in my head.
Will this ever come to an end?
I shall never know, my friend.

Deep in thought, drifting in space,
A mystery to the human race.

Miles Stickler (13)
Perryfields High School, Oldbury

MEN ARE . . .

Men are stupid and think they're all it,
Men just dig themselves into a pit,
They always lie and take everything as a joke,
It makes me sick and makes me choke.

I don't know why they were ever created,
I really can't see how we're possibly related,
They always want to be rough and have a tumble
And never consider being lenient and humble.

Men are dumb and walk like chimps,
They stutter around with their brains in links,
Most of the crime is caused by men,
They can't drive cars and can't count to ten.

Men always think they're strong and hard,
But when it comes to fighting their heads turn to lard,
They drink all day at local pubs,
But when they're finished can't pay the subs.

Men have always eaten like pigs
And leave the women to clean away the cigs,
I wish they would all go away
'Cause if they don't we'll all turn gay,
They are hopeless and useless and all cause wars,
Men are filthy, men are bores.

Men ignore what women see,
We should call it 'her story'.

Gemma Normansell (15)
Perryfields High School, Oldbury

What It's Like To Be Homeless

It's sad and it's upsetting
And certainly no fun.
People look at you
Like a criminal on the run.

I'm put in all conditions,
Whether it be sun, wind or rain.
The things people do and say
Cause me a great deal of pain.

I don't like living on the streets
But it's better than going back there.
People don't realise what it's like
To be put into care.

I never imagined my life
To be like this.
All I want is someone to love me,
Hug and kiss.

My life is boring
And will never be great.
My heart always has and always will
Be full of hate.

If you're considering
Leaving home,
Think again,
Do you really want to be alone?

Lucy Edwards (15)
Perryfields High School, Oldbury

Running a Film Backwards

The sick dog

I was lying on the table
With my eyes shut,
Calling out for Mabel,
Another mutt.

I was at home
All alone,
No one there to look after me
Why couldn't they hear my plea?

There I was, playing fetch.
Running around
Making lots of sound,
Finally, someone loved me.

I'm six today
Getting a bit too old to play,
Everyone's fussing around me
Which was nice to see.

I'm a fast little scamp,
I even managed to knock over the lamp,
I'm a happy puppy
They called me Sooty.

Out I came, into the world
Making lots of noise,
My tail all curled,
I was happy.

Jessica Lloyd (11)
Summerhill School, Kingswinford

THE TURKEY'S LIFE BACKWARDS

It's Christmas Day!
I'm on someone's plate,
I'm going to be eaten,
Is it really to be!

The factory's working backwards,
I'm being unpacked.
My feathers are here,
There's just one thing I lack.

I'm back in that shed
Where I'm gruesomely killed.
The axe is back up,
I feel great and refilled.

I'm back in the farmyard,
It's just turned December.
I'm getting quite cold,
It'll soon be September.

I'm just a little chick now
And I'll soon be an egg,
So now it's time to say
Goodbye until we meet again.

James Willetts (11)
Summerhill School, Kingswinford

THE CARING OLD WOMAN

This face in front of me is old and worn,
You may see another born.
I see her wrinkles, like a crinkled leaf,
Her smiling mouth drawn up to her white teeth.

I see her lips like a line,
They are a bit like mine.
She has grey, curly, bushy hair,
You can see she's full of care.

Her squinted eyes, which are blue,
You can see them straight through.
This woman is full of love,
She is like a sweet little dove.

Charlotte Baker (12)
Summerhill School, Kingswinford

A TREE

They picked me up
And taped me straight
They stood back and looked
And had tea in a cup

The humble age of 100
Has crept silently up on me
Soon I will be young again
And full of childish glee

Now at the age of 20
I feel the wind and snow
I have a big food supply
Which I will use till winter may go

Friends are growing taller
Streets are growing wider
Children try and pick me up
But I'm about to meet my maker

I'm stuck up here
On this rotten tree
All my friends are massive
And wonder what I'll be . . .

Thomas Cleeton (11)
Summerhill School, Kingswinford

A POEM ABOUT A TREE

Here I am standing alone and cold
My leaves have disappeared off me
they were my clothes.

Here I am standing with my tree friends
happily with my clothes,
but they are ready, very ready, to drop off me and
I will be naked again.

Here I am standing tall and proud,
with the other trees.
I'm ready to work again, make food for myself
and I'm sucking water up through my roots.

Here I am, medium-sized, not all fully grown yet,
but I'm getting there, I'm growing my leaves
to make food for myself.

Here I am, small and not developed yet,
I haven't even managed to grow my first leaf at all.

Here I am in bud on my mum's tree where
I will drop off soon and start growing.

Samantha Beddows (11)
Summerhill School, Kingswinford

MYSTERIOUS OLD MAN

This face is a mystery
holds many secrets and adventure,
Whitewashed up, willowy hair
looking like a burrowing bull.

This face has a talent
he looks kind, and a friend to everyone.
Accompanying animals and accomplishing many great journeys
looking like bark on a tree.

This face is a poor soul
he looks alone, in his own world.
We look at him as a precipitated, precise, polar bear,
as sad as the night sky.

A restriction and confliction.

Stewart Herbert (12)
Summerhill School, Kingswinford

A LAUGH

It used to be a happy time,
It sounded like a chime
The glee, the pleasure
It is beyond measure.

First it was a snigger,
Then swelled, did the figure.
The mouth did open
The laugh was spoken

The child stood there dumbfounded,
As the joke was there, now founded.
His sides did split
As if they were fit.

The joke was so original
It was just a signal
For greater happiness it made
Which will never fade.

Before all this, the sadness
The laughter brought some gladness
So all around the sadness
Was engulfed by the gladness.

Adam Bottley (11)
Summerhill School, Kingswinford

THE TREE LIFE

The tree, all rotten and broken in two,
Is getting younger, minute by minute.
Yet there it is, the mould all gone
And healing its wounds.

It's ten years gone,
Life's getting better
Children playing upon its branches.

People using its shelter from the rain,
It's feeling much better now, it's younger
Still growing younger, younger, younger.

Now it's just a little bit -
Only a stick, standing in the ground,
But still it's getting smaller.
They stand and stare at what will become
Of this little tree

And when they've gone, its life's just started.
A little seed burrowed underground.
Life's all new, what can it do?

Pippa Smith (11)
Summerhill School, Kingswinford

THE LOVELY OLD WOMAN

I can see her old face beginning to have some peace,
I can see her hard, rough wrinkles, like a crinkled leaf.
Her smiling mouth drawn up to her white teeth,
I see her nose, like a bike horn
Her face is a lovely picture of warmth.

I see her great big blue eyes, like the sea,
Her hair so fine is what I can see.
Her lips are so straight, like a long line,
I can tell she is very kind.

Her hair is a fluffy tail
And her skin colour is so pale.
This woman has a lot of love,
She is like a little, white dove.

Michaela Banner (12)
Summerhill School, Kingswinford

THE TREE

1,000 years old
the oldest you ever did see,
at the moment I'm chunky and bald
the most ugliest tree.

All my branches are bent
but my leaves are still pretty,
although I have a little dirt
I am in the middle of the city.

I am bushy and bright
I am very kind,
beautiful and light.
A shame for anybody who's blind.

I am as tiny as ever I could be,
why, why, why?
Everybody keeps sitting on me
if only I was not shy.

Sunshine and water
it makes my day,
a drop of water will soon shoot up
please make me a beautiful tree,
I pray.

Ria Aldersley (11)
Summerhill School, Kingswinford

MUGSHOTS!

Old and wrinkly
looks bubbly and still fresh.

Eyes are tiny
looking for something far away.

Brings out an expression which is happy
and successful, but sometimes *sad!*

Teeth are all white and clean
her teeth cannot be missed anywhere.
So shiny! So clean!

Her hair is very fair and soft,
just sitting on a smooth head.
firm and full of feelings,
and important information.

Here eyebrows, full of joy
and happiness.

Nose round, but a little bit
pointed at the end,
which makes her face look like
a witch's nose.

Stephanie Richards (12)
Summerhill School, Kingswinford

ALL ABOUT A GIRL'S MUGSHOTS

The girl's face has the look of evil,
her eyes tell us that she is about to do something wrong.
She acts like she knows everything and is rough and strong
her facial expressions say it all -
that she is just going to stand tall.
She walks around like she doesn't care,
people walking and standing, having a stare.

She is a woman in disguise as a man, and
people wondering, is that person a woman or a man?
People thinking, is she horrible or mean?
But really, she's lonely and keen.
Her hair looks like rough sandpaper,
when you feel it, you get a funny
feeling on your hand.

Louise Walters (13)
Summerhill School, Kingswinford

THE DOG, OLD TO YOUNG

The dog it is old,
Twenty years old, not knowing what to do,
He is too old to play,
Lying in his basket all day.

He's getting younger day by day,
Still getting tired each time he runs,
He's still getting a walk twice in twenty-four hours,
Walking in the flowers.

It's his fifteenth birthday, it's raining,
So he won't get a nice walk today,
He wonders if his owners will take him for a walk at all,
So he will have to lie in his basket just looking at his ball.

He's still getting younger each day,
He's now playing with his ball,
Nine years old, having children playing with him all day,
When he is on holiday, gets a walk by the bay.

He's a puppy all sweet and soft,
The children can't stop playing with him,
He's still thinking where he came from,
He thinks back and sees his mommy and him.

Laura Jackson (11)
Summerhill School, Kingswinford

MUGSHOTS

Her skin is as soft as silk,
there's a hint of a smile
opening on her face
her eyes slightly
looking at the side, as if she's upset.

The make-up washes away
her young beautiful skin,
as she looks bothered by
her appearance.

Her expensive earrings
shine in the light like
a cool diamond.

Her long, silky hair
is softened in the wind.

Her clothes are richly embroidered
in smooth, gold thread.

She looks timid and shy
like she doesn't want to shout.
She's proud of who she is
with her jewellery and clothes.
She likes to show her religion upon her face.

Catherine Hollies (12)
Summerhill School, Kingswinford

RUNNING A FILM BACKWARDS

My backwards life:

Back in the stable, with my eyes shut
I knew what was wrong with my foot.
I can feel the straw in the dark,
I can hear the fireworks go with a spark.

For the last few days I couldn't move,
I could hear the sounds of someone's shoes.
They were bringing the food which horses hate,
But for me, it is simply great.

At the age of an adult
I knew, with riding, I'd have a good result.
I was then at the age of a champion
And I knew that my mom would come.

Still getting younger at the age of a youth,
I knew over my head, I would have a new roof.
Then at the age of five,
I knew I would walk for my life.

I'm lying down in the straw
With my mom, more and more.
Now I'm in a place I can't describe,
I wonder who I am inside?

Emily McLachlan (11)
Summerhill School, Kingswinford

THE OLD MAN

The man looks weak
he has fluff on his cheek.
He has a long beard
he looks quite weird.
He has pointed eyebrows
like demon cows.
His face is crinkled, like a crisp
he may have a lisp.
His eyes are droopy like
a dog called Poopy.
He might be bald,
the strange man called.

He looks really poor
like an old rotting door,
He smells dead,
he's whacking his head.
He has a wide nose and
might be a Hobo!
He looks quite friendly
but could be deadly.
He looks happy
like Scooby and Scrappy.
His hair is white,
he doesn't want to fight.

Adam Ankers (12)
Summerhill School, Kingswinford

MUGSHOTS

Her face is like a smooth
soft piece of silk,
with the shape of an oval peach.

Her lips look full,
there isn't a trace of a smile.
Here eyebrows look wide
and bushy.
Her eyes look shocked,
as she looks at you.

Her ears are placed by the side of her face,
with her large, dazzling earrings
attached to them.

Her nose looks straight
and pointed.
Her hair looks solid,
stiff and secure.
When the wind blows it,
it doesn't move.

The colour of her hair is brown,
with a tiny reflection of light.
Her clothes look smart and tidy -
but her life looks unhappy.

Ellie Nimmo (12)
Summerhill School, Kingswinford

THE MATCH IN REVERSE

The match had finished 5-0
at Wembley Stadium on a
rainy day.

The players scored goals
and came out uninjured.

It went down to 4-0
One yellow card was given to a player
for going in two-footed.

The subs came on for the injured player.
He flew backwards in the air
and then flipped sideways.

3-0 now. The crowd is going mad
because it was in with a chip.

Now it is 2-0, with a
kick to the side.

1-0 now and the players
have just started.
The crowd are not singing
very loudly.

Now the match has started at 0-0
the time is 3.40pm.

Christopher Motteram (12)
Summerhill School, Kingswinford

RUN THE FILM BACKWARDS

Spinning round in circles,
Round and round he goes,
He's just been dropped in the toilet,
He's dead now he knows.

Then suddenly he's in his tank,
Swimming round quite slow,
That big old fish is nearly dead
So he's swimming quite low.

Now he's swimming fast again
Like a little fish,
He's suddenly just shrunk in size,
He never made a wish.

Then suddenly he's in a bag
As a passenger in a car,
There are people all around him,
He fears they're driving far.

Now he's in a shop again
With people glaring in,
There are fish all around him,
Peeking at his fin.

But now he's in a dark place,
It looks just like a hall.
Then he comes shooting out
And crashes into a wall.

Richard Mansell (11)
Summerhill School, Kingswinford

RUNNING THE FILM BACKWARDS

So here I am at sixty-five,
old, weak and grey.
At least I know I'm still alive
and that I'll safely lay.

Fifty eh! Oh my life!
I'll be retiring soon.
After all that hard work and strife,
I'll soon be resting in the womb.

I've got three children, don't know how!
must have had a man.
I'm twenty now
Whoo! Yippee! I'm young and I think, free.

Cool dude, hip thirteen
jeans, bring it on.
I'm a groove teen
A top totty queen.

Ahh! Cute, I know I am
in my dungarees,
Mom says I'm a sweet little lamb
and should stay just the same.

Laid to peace in the womb
comfortably lying
what will I be when I'm born again?

Laura Pearson (12)
Summerhill School, Kingswinford

THE CAT, OLD TO YOUNG

It's dark and I am cold,
I am twenty years old and I am not up to doing anything.
Where am I?
I'm lying pale and blue in my place where I was buried.
Help!
They're holding me with their cold, wet hands.

I'm getting younger as the days go by,
I am lying by the gentle fire
That is lit by the wonderful decorative fireplace.
They all say, 'Look at that cat sitting by the fire.
I suppose that's all cats do, eat, drink and sleep.'
I'm thinking that it won't be long till I'm playing with my toys.

I'm ten years old, I have my own litter,
Soon I will be saying goodbye to them
And seeing me their age.
My owner cares for me and my owner also loves kittens,
She would do anything for us!
Even when I'm this age I still think of my mum.

I am just a kitten,
My fur all soft and fluffy.
My sisters are over there and so are my toys.
My ears are perked up and my eyes are bright
As I hear my owner get food for tea,
But sometimes I still want my mum.

Alexandra D'Silva (11)
Summerhill School, Kingswinford

MY BAND

When I was an old man,
I was married, when she took me upstairs,
I was carried.

At the age of sixty-five
We built up our band and then it died,
We all split up,
I wonder why?

The best age is thirty-two
Because our band was famous.
My drum kit grew enormous
And every girl thought I was gorgeous.

Twenty-one is the next best age
Because we went on a tour of Britain
And when I was there I bought a cage
Because I'd bought a kitten.

When I was only thirteen
My hands were really hurting.
My hands had blisters on them
Because we played loads of gigs.

When I was a little boy,
In fact I was only six
And my band hadn't started
Because I had no sticks.

Callum Maclean (11)
Summerhill School, Kingswinford

THE GOAT

Lying still
no heart to hear
Billy Goat Gruff
has died

Turn back time
erase the past
Billy's old and feeble
see him struggle to stand

Years of time go back
a middle-aged goat
A father too
walks with his loving wife.

Here we see a goat in his prime
standing with his head up high,
Butting people
aiming for the sky.

Here is a kid
foolish and weak,
He trips over a stone
giving a bleat.

Back in the womb
safe as can be
Rejoined with his mother
no danger to see.

Alicia Hand (12)
Summerhill School, Kingswinford

RUN THE LIFE BACKWARDS

I'm lying here in a coffin
As cold as stone
I'm waiting to be buried
I'm going to turn to bone

I'm getting younger by the minute
I am only going to see
That I have a husband
This really can't be

Now I'm at the age of 40
What is happening to me?
I have two 20-year-old children
I can't believe what I can see

Now I'm 30
It's my birthday you see
Half these people I don't know
But they're my husband's friends, you see

I'm now 16
I have met my love
He's really cute
I don't remember this at all

I'm in my mum's tummy
I'm bouncing around
I'm scared about coming out
I know I've got to grow up . . .

Claire Coley (12)
Summerhill School, Kingswinford

THE OLD WOMAN

This face in front, is old and drawn
Her smile fills her with warmth
The wrinkles are so worn
Her nose is just like a horn.

Her eyes so blue, I can see the ocean through
Her teeth are just like the whitest cloud.
Her lips, so fine
Her hair is grey, just like the bay.

She is as nice as you think
Her skin is very pink
As she blinks, a second has gone by.

Abbie Leah Cooper (12)
Summerhill School, Kingswinford

MUGSHOTS

Her eyes are as sharp as knives,
Her eyebrows, sharp and dainty
like razor blades.

You would think she was a man -
but the two earrings give her away.

But inside, she is lonely and longing
for someone to hold and love her.

Kim Davis (12)
Summerhill School, Kingswinford

CHOCOLATE MONSTER

When I saw it, it gave me a fright,
Right in the corner, out went the light.
'Aarrgghh!' I screamed and hid under my sheets,
Was I to be the monster's next meal?

Had it gone? That question was still in my mind,
If I took off the sheets, what would I find?
I pushed them off and looked around,
There he was, on the ground.

'What do you want? I have no meat,
You are very welcome to take a seat.'
The monster replied, 'I am a chocolate beast,
Chocolate, all sorts, is my kind of feast.

If you wish to see your mother someday,
Three bars of chocolate is the price you will pay.'
I handed it over and he gave me my mother,
What a shame that it hadn't been my brother!

Hannah Owen (11)
Thomas Telford School, Telford

MY GRANNY HAS AN OLD BANGER

My granny has an old banger
It's blue with purple spots
She keeps a portable telly in there
And watches Top Of The Pops!

My granny has an old banger
She drives it so very quick
Everyone who rides in it
Becomes severely sick.

My granny has an old banger
She sold it for a quid
She went into the fishmongers
And asked them for a squid.

Claire Louise Sutton (11)
Thomas Telford School, Telford

REVOLVING DOOR

Spinning around every day,
Every season come what may.
People pushing me, coming in and out,
I dizzily watch people about.
Everyone different in every way
I listen carefully to what they say.

A group of women striding into the shop,
One of them wondering whether to buy a new top.
Ladies covered from head to toe
With sapphires, diamonds on show.
Frantic men, shopping on Christmas Eve,
Buying all their presents before they leave.
Children moaning, screaming for toys,
Coming out happy little girls and boys.
Everyone different in every way,
I listen carefully to what they say.

As my switch goes off and the lights go down,
The room is empty, not even a sound.
It's time to rest after a long day,
Everyone different in every way.
I've listened carefully to what they . . .
Zzzzzzzzz

Natalie Picken (11)
Thomas Telford School, Telford

THE TWIN TOWERS

Everything was still and everything was peaceful,
The birds were singing,
The bees were buzzing,
Everything was perfect.

Everything was still and everything was peaceful,
But that was no longer,
The Earth stood at a standstill watching,
Waiting for their nightmare to finish.

In it went, piercing through and it parked there and stayed,
People were running,
People were crying
And I could not believe it.

Then there was another,
It was like a video tape that had been rewound,
As I watched it again a tear fell down,
I just stared and did not believe.

When it collapsed
I lost my breath,
I was no longer in my living room but in New York,
Down it went, down, down, down.

Then the other one went,
What was happening?
I just didn't know,
I just didn't understand.

All of those lives,
All of the feelings,
All of their families.

I must live
And we must all keep their memories alive.

Kirsty Ford (13)
Thomas Telford School, Telford

THE MOST EXCITING WEEK

On Monday I went to the zoo
And I saw a kangaroo
I said, 'Boo!'
And the kangaroo
Jumped halfway out of the zoo.

On Tuesday I went to the fair
And I won a teddy bear.
I named the bear
After my sister Claire,
But she didn't like it, so she pulled my hair.

On Wednesday I went to the park
And I met my boyfriend, Mark.
My boyfriend Mark
Had a dog called Bark,
Who ran around the park.

On Thursday I went to the games arcade,
And I made a mate, his name was Ade.
We each had a cup of lemonade
And then some toast with marmalade,
Which went quite well with the lemonade.

On Friday I went to the swimming pool,
Where I met a silly fool.
The silly fool thought he was cool
And said so, so I pushed him in the pool.
So then he broke a very strict rule.

On Saturday I stayed at home,
Most of the time I was on the phone
But I had to get off to give my dog a bone.

But what happened on Sunday . . . ?

Becky Brown (11)
Thomas Telford School, Telford

THE OLD FARM GATE

My mommy took me out one day
To see where all the animals play
Sheep and goats and horses too
All on the farm with Mr Minchew.

I was happy sitting there,
On the porch in the farmer's chair.
Watching the ducks playing by the pond
I wish this day would be very long.

It's time to leave, it's 5pm
The farmer's here, with all his men.
My mommy says, 'It's getting late.'

I wish I could swing on the old farm gate.

Hollie Goodreid (11)
Thomas Telford School, Telford

FOOTBALL FINAL

The crowd roared like a wild animal
As I stepped up to the big challenge
My heart was beating rapidly
I ran towards the ball like a cheetah in full flight
Searching swerving, searching for the net
I thought will it go in, will it not?
Yes, no, yes
Smack! The ball hits the net
Shouts from the crowd I will never forget
The glory then hit me.

Alex Harnett (13)
Thomas Telford School, Telford

MY MAGIC BOX

(Based on 'Magic Box' by Kit Wright)

I will store in my box:
The gracefulness of the enchanting blue whale;
The magical look of the gold-horned unicorn;
The silver shimmer of a crystal cloud.

I will force into my box:
The gleam of Excalibur's blade in the sun;
The clash of glitter as kings' armaments meet;
The glowing bronze of a Roman's battle shield.

My box is fashioned from burning icicles and Aztec emeralds;
With flashing thunderbolts for nails and dragon teeth to bind it;
Its handles are beautiful rainbows.

I shall go deep in my box, deep to the bottom of the sea
Where the peaceful dolphins play.
Then up, high up into the dreams of the moon.

Daniel Yeo (12)
Thomas Telford School, Telford

MY AUTUMN POEM

I feel the wind's gentle hand stroke the hair upon my head
I see the wind blow the leaves into a great swirl of brown and red
I smell the wind as it carries the scent of a newly baked apple pie
I hear the wind howl, then calm, then die.

Thomas Stentiford (12)
Thomas Telford School, Telford

SHOPPING!

The car pulls into the nearest space
We all jump out
Me, Louise, and Grace.
Grab the trolley, put Louise in the seat
Glance at the list,
'Darling, add on bread and meat.'

In bright letters, away up high
ASDA is written
Shining in the sky.
Whilst Mum's heaven, it is our doom
We're dragged inside
A morning of gloom.

Five hours later, behind a mountain of food
After getting all the way round
We were in a very bad mood.
Mum, however, was happy enough,
'Cheer up' she laughed,
'No more shopping until next month!'

Charlotte Burton (11)
Thomas Telford School, Telford

SPRING

When she comes the flowers will grow,
A beautiful array of daffodils will show.
As she swoops over trees and flowers,
She works on her spring beauties for hours and hours.

As she works, the flowers become brighter and brighter,
And the winter days become lighter and lighter.
As she does her spring dance
The flowers drift into a magical trance.

She will not leave until her work is complete,
But then the summer will soon delete.
The beautiful work which spring has done
To make way for the summer sun.

Rebecca Buttery (11)
Thomas Telford School, Telford

THE GOLDEN HAND

There I stand
With the ring in my hand,
I look all around
And see lions on the ground.
Young and old, they roar out loud
All I can hear is a high-pitched sound.
My stomach has flutters
And my words have stutters.
I run with the ring
When I see something.
I strike with my right
And everything seems bright.
I throw the ring
As it lands with a ping
The Devil steps aside,
My goal is open wide.
The sticks fall to the ground
As there is a loud sound.
Everyone is running
And says, 'That was stunning!'
All around me I have glory
As I retell everyone the story.

Paramveer Gill (11)
Thomas Telford School, Telford

A TASTE OF FEAR

I stand there,
Staring.
Staring at the door.
Sweat dripping down,
Down my forehead.
I hold my heart in my hands,
Summoning enough courage
To move forward,
To open the door!
My hand shaking as I reach out,
Reach out for the handle,
To turn it, to open the door.
It opens.
Hairs standing up on my spine,
My heart ready to burst.
I cannot go on.
I cannot move forward,
Frozen to the spot with fear!

Lewis Adcock (11)
Thomas Telford School, Telford

AUTUMN

Leaves, they fall to the ground
Softly, silently, not making a sound.
All different colours of oranges and red,
Scattered at our feet, like a blanket on a bed.

Autumn is here. Autumn is here.
Here are things that tell us autumn is here . . .

On goes the wellies, the scarves and the hats.
The children are playing with their balls and their bats.
People are hurrying to their homes before dark
Or watching the bonfires set up in the park.

Autumn is here. Autumn is here.
These are the things that tell us autumn is here.

Nadia Bobash (11)
Thomas Telford School, Telford

GLORY?

My foot came down on the explosion-scorched earth,
A rancid smell of death around me.
A thousand deaths, for what it's worth.
Is this what they do for glory?

The charred remains of innocent lives, cut down in all their prime
Contorted faces that would make the Devil himself weep.
Calling up the fires of Hell, into our modern time.
Tormented souls, for evermore, tortured in their sleep.

Quiet, concrete, cosy homes demolished in a blast
Quiet, cosy, loving homes built and made to last.
Dirty sun, blasted earth, polluted river flows by
Market stalls and kiddies' parks gone in the blink of an eye.

A thousand deaths, for what it's worth.
This is what they do for glory.

Sean Weston (16)
Thomas Telford School, Telford

FOOTBALL FAD

A little boy called Alex Finch
Loved football more than life
He only wished to volley balls
He didn't want a wife!

To play for Man U was his dream
As Beckham's number seven
Nothing else passed through his mind
He thought he was in Heaven.

He'd think about it day and night
And drive his parents bonkers
They worried he'd become a geek
They'd rather he played conkers!

The walls got cracked, the floors did shake
From all his football training
The neighbours hoped he'd stop the noise
What relief when it was raining!

One day he woke and realised
That football was just a game
He'd rather have a game of pool
Oh what a terrible shame!

Alex Finch (11)
Thomas Telford School, Telford

A WITCH

A witch is a dark purple and black
She is the autumn
On a broomstick
She is rainy and cold

A witch is a cloak and hat
She is an old couch
She is 'The Simpsons Hallowe'en Special'
A witch is a candy apple.

Fodoulla Vanezi (12)
Thomas Telford School, Telford

CHARLIE THE CRICKETING CAT

Charlie's so good at cricket
He loves to hit the wicket,
He's really a wonderful cat
A true wizard with the bat.
Charlie, the cricketing cat.

He plays for the Lancs,
Sponsored by Barclays Bank.
Charlie always wears whites
And never bites.
Charlie, the cricketing cat.

He's better than the rest
Of course, he is the best,
His friend's a donkey
And his bat's all wonky.
Charlie, the cricketing cat.

He scores lots of sixes and fours
With his really useful paws.
A win, it will surely be
As Charlie scores another century.
Charlie, the cricketing cat.

Daniel Loftus (11)
Thomas Telford School, Telford

THE WASTED TREE OF LIFE

The tree of life stood hanging
Over the busy world below
Stood tall in the summer sky
Above the people yet to know

Then one single day in autumn
When nobody even knew
A dreadful thing happened
Hiding war which was to brew

A few seconds of not thinking
The world began to shake
The tree of life came falling
A bed of leaves to make

Then winter arrived sooner
The sky was left all bare
Many lives have been wasted
How could someone dare?

Spring was slow to arrive
The rebuilding of lives
How brave some people were
Leaving widowed children and wives

Now a year has passed
The ruins cleared away
The images still in our hearts
As we live another day

September 11 2001.

Louise Shenton (13)
Thomas Telford School, Telford

A DAY TRIP TO FRANCE

Looking forward to it for ages
And today was the day
We were going to France, it was quite a long way
To Folkestone, to catch Le Shuttle
A lot of people and one big, scary, brown train

To wait in the long queue, we eventually drove on
Then into the deep black tunnel and gone
To arrive in Calais, it was a sight to see
Inside the shops, it was really busy
The pubs and cafés were as full as can be

The French are very different in everything they do
From fashion to food, no matter what it is
Just say 'Bonjour!' and I'm sure they'll say it to you
On the road, you can tell that you're in France
Because in their cars, they'll just whizz past.

I'm starving, what's there to eat I wonder?
Pizza, yum yum, with a glass of Coke and
Ice cream for pudding.
Buying in Euros; it's too confusing
Presents for friends and chocolate for me
Speaking in French (not that much!)

I'm really tired and thirsty
We stop for a while; I get a drink
I fall asleep and then wake up
Finally, we get home
I look at the time
It's midnight; I'm going to bed.

Charlotte Proud (11)
Thomas Telford School, Telford

MY GRANDAD

My grandad is quite an eccentric
He tinkers with cars all day
He loves them almost as much
As children love to play

He loves to go back in time
Aided by his 'Old Glory' magazine
His favourite television programme
Is (you've guessed it) 'Time Team'!

He used to work at Sankeys
An electrician by trade;
But when he retired, his skills didn't fail
Often coming to people's aid.

Steam engines are his hobby
Along with trains and mending cars;
And after a hard day in the garage
His treat is a few chocolate bars!

I love him to recall his school days
Air raids and wearing gas masks;
And his favourite teacher Mr Ferriday
Setting him numerous hard tasks.

My grandad used to play the drums
In various local bands
I'd love him to teach me one day
With his skilful, talented hands.

I love my grandad very much
That is why I wrote this poem;
And I hope that when you read it
You think you'd like to know him.

Charlotte Hughes (11)
Thomas Telford School, Telford

Owl

Silent as a glider
The owl swoops by
Knowing the bright moon
Is nigh.

Now he's collected
For a feast,
Quite enough
For his family, at least.

Lily-white against
The ebony sky,
The owl returns home
Bedtime is close by.

As morning dawns
The owl rests
In his retreat,
As others rise from their nests.

He perches in the tree,
Sleeping off the flight,
Preparing himself to hunt
The following night.

The owl sleeps silently
Whilst others start to sing.
But he knows he'll have
A great time, hunting on the wing.

Kellyann Shorter (11)
Thomas Telford School, Telford

HALLOWE'EN

The autumn months are cold and dark,
Especially at night,
We all dress up for Hallowe'en
And give ourselves a fright.

Ghosts and ghouls are everywhere,
As well as witches with long wiry hair,
Skeletons with eyes aglow,
Open the window and watch the show.

Granny gets a shock again
When she hears that knock,
She opens the door and falls right back
After nearly getting a smack.

Pumpkins grin with their creepy smile
Leading the light for over a mile,
So watch out on Hallowe'en
Lots of people will give you a scream.

Ian Rowlands (11)
Thomas Telford School, Telford

BABY JESUS

When I think of Jesus' childhood
there's something that I must get straight.
If there wasn't a Christmas Day
He would have nothing to celebrate.

He didn't have a Christmas tree,
with tinsel and lots of lights.
But I bet He and His mother Mary
were so happy, they slept at night.

She probably made Him a lovely cake
with the candles that all glow.
And little Jesus made a wish
blew them out, in just one blow.

Little Jesus' friends had come
with presents they would bring.
They had no carols in those days
what on earth were they going to sing?

Casey Skillen (11)
Thomas Telford School, Telford

MY FIRST DAY AT SECONDARY SCHOOL

As I got out the car and said goodbye
I looked at the big kids and got shy
It was like a new place
In outer space
My first lesson was tech
I got in a real wreck
Halfway through we had breakfast
There were a lot of rooms we passed
After tech we went to PT
Which is nothing like DT
When I went to science
I thought I had to have a licence
After lunch
We got in a bunch
We did some more science
Without a licence
Then we went home
To get a comb.

Danny Lindley (11)
Thomas Telford School, Telford

THE HIROSHIMA BOMB

Screams and shouts of distress filled the city of Hiroshima,
Hundreds of people crying, confused, looking in amazement
At each other
The city, once so full of life, had suddenly changed into a bleak, dull,
Grey, lifeless place.
The question *why?* on people's faces.

People missing, injured, dead.
Trees, rivers, wildlife fled,
Homes and buildings destroyed
People hear the news of their family and friends they want to avoid
And people are still asking, why?

Why such mass destruction?
Why an atomic bomb?
Why are innocent people killed?
Why, what have we done?

Hannah Wilcox (15)
Thomas Telford School, Telford

UNFORGOTTEN

Tears rolling down your cheeks,
Voice which quivers, limbs so weak.
Hoping, wishing to share your pain
Upon my heart, that day shall stain

Your smile displayed your growing pride,
You took each knock-back in your stride.
Every second was a memory I'd endeavour,
How I thought you'd last forever.

But like all good stories, the book must end,
A broken heart is unable to mend.
Tears clean an open wound,
Goodbyes approach, yet forsooned.

A young child gazing up so high,
Staring at the midnight sky.
Joyful tears will fall, I'm not sure when,
As we are reunited once again.

Joanna Codling (13)
Thomas Telford School, Telford

I Am The Real IRA

Catholic deprivation of rights and freedom urged me to join
The decision to terrorise was at the flip of a coin
Explosives: my field of interest to the IRA
People were soon to swoon from my triumphant explosive array!

Revulsion for the Catholic race
Soon the day will come for the Unionists to splinter into waste.
A faction of honour and pride
Through the city of Omagh the IRA shall ride!

What glory do the Unionists have?
For their soldiers stand drib and drab.
With an army of hundreds the IRA will prevail
For the City of Omagh will rain with kinetic nails.

Frustrated with Loyalists' excess force on innocent Catholic affirmation
The Paramilitary can't help being ruthless murderers. No obligation
So in Omagh on its date we all will pray
To live on another day.
For I am the Real IRA.

Selim Dayanik (15)
Thomas Telford School, Telford

STAINED GRAVES

Stationed fearful, under the bomb enduring the persistent
Smells and sounds and crashes of the costly bombing.
Men's cries from outside can be heard echoing enthusiastically
Through the wall
Making it harder for brave hearts to emerge.

Seconds seem like minutes,
Minutes seem like hours.
My life passes before me,
Where can I turn?
Shall I run the gauntlet of heroes or
Face the punishment of cowards?

Death comes to all of us!
But we wonder what title will stain our grave
After many husbands, brothers and sons have been
Lost through years of battling!

Henry Goh (15)
Thomas Telford School, Telford

MURDER

Why do we do it?
Why don't we think, choose forgiveness,
Then pursue it?
We often choose the hard road,
Though it's as easy as a game of football -
Here mate, on your head,
Shoot the gun and now you're dead, ha ha!
Then, the next day it's all over the court.
Is it only then
That we realise how dearly that bullet was bought?

Philip Bailey (13)
Thomas Telford School, Telford

My New Bike!

I got my first bike when I was 5.
It was pink and it had four wheels.
I couldn't wait to ride it, so I took it for a spin.
I charged it around the block,
I rode it so fast; I was like a leopard.
But as I turned the corner, the bike screamed at me,
I screamed and *smash!*
I fell on a piece of glass.
It went into my leg and cut me open,
Like I was having an operation.
I screamed for help.

I hopped in pain,
My dad came out and picked me up and
He shut up my wound and made me better,
Thanks Dad!

Natalie Bayliss (14)
Thomas Telford School, Telford

A True Friend

A true friend is honest and kind
They're always there when I'm in a bind
They're funny, they're happy, they make me laugh
And most of mine, are just plain daft

There is only one true friend I call the best
She is caring, sharing, a bit more than the rest
I'd hate to think that this was the end
Cos I don't know what I'd do if
I was to lose my best friend.

Ceri Jones (11)
Thomas Telford School, Telford

SPOOKY SPELL

Hubble, scubble,
Cauldron bubble.
Eye of newt,
Dead man's toe,
Put this in with a great big throw.
Hubble, scubble,
Cauldron bubble,
Turn him into a frog
And make it double.

Two fat children,
One fat male.
Stick in a whale
And a dragon's scale.
A pinch of dust,
A dead man's toe.
Give it a stir
And what do you know?

Careful it's hot!
You might have to blow.
A lot of hard work,
But worth it though.
Eat it all up,
But please don't throw up!

Sarah Vernon (11)
Thomas Telford School, Telford

STARS

Look at the stars, they are so bright,
Why do they only shine at night?
Why don't they sparkle all day long?
Where they truly do belong.

Why aren't they here when I'm awake?
I love the silvery light they make.
I wish upon the first one's glare
And pray they'll always be up there.

Philip Liebman (11)
Thomas Telford School, Telford

THEY ARE THERE

My inspiration is not just one man,
But a group of men.
These men fight for the right,
Fight for the right until the night.
These men are men of honour
And which are praised by millions.
These men work hard and never disappoint.
When their country calls for them
They are there.
When their country is fighting for a holy grail,
These men are there.
The men that are in this team
Are captained by a man that is an idol to all.
With him is a man small in stature,
But huge in heart and courage.
Also, someone that when they are in trouble,
He will clear the danger away.
Together, these three men
Joined with nine other elites from around the world,
Produced an unstoppable force.
These are my idols,
These are the kings,
These are always there.
The England football squad.

Nicholas Nicholson (13)
Thomas Telford School, Telford

OPERATION

Just turned four, a sister just arrived
Operation eyeball was the next thing for me.

Off to Shrewsbury I was sent
To see the doctor that would make me pretty again
A time, a date, they were all set
An operation was a sure bet
To fix my eye, he would do his best and to get rid of all that mess.

Some medicine and a gown I had
A ride on the trolley I was promised
If I wasn't naughty or mad.

Winnie the Pooh I had to hold, whilst the doctor, not that old,
Told me I was tired and needed a sleep
And to make sure that I didn't peek,

When I woke I couldn't see, a spoonful of Calpol they gave to me
My eyes were fixed, but would be sore
But cysts I would have no more
Drops and medicines I took home
But when Mum gave them to me I did moan
My eyes are fixed and even though I look so pretty
The needle for the doc I could stick where he sits.

Ruth Moorhouse (13)
Thomas Telford School, Telford

I WISH YOU!

Prickles and slugs,
Boils and bugs,
That's what I wish you.

A kick in the face,
A punch in the waist
And a pinch on the arm too.

Keep out of sight,
For fear that I might
Give you a bleeding nose.

Don't show your face
Around any place,
Or you'll have me on your case!

Katie Harris (12)
Thomas Telford School, Telford

AN AWFUL WAR

You can close your eyes and try to imagine
The horrors of this awful war
Dead bodies lie scattered in the mud
The ground covered in a blanket of blood

You can try to imagine the noises
The noises of this awful war
Coughs from the poison gas, soldiers choking
Repetitive gunshots drumming in the soldiers' ears

You can try to imagine the sights
The sights of this awful war
Shot down men left to die in the mud
Men in the trenches left ill with trench foot

You can try to imagine the pain
The agonies of this awful war
Blinding soldiers like babies, totally dependant on others
Soldiers sinking, choking, unable to find aid

You can close your eyes and try to imagine
The horrors of this awful war
But, you can't, the shocking truth is surreal
Unless, you have been in this awful, awful war.

Natalie Ball (13)
Thomas Telford School, Telford

TIDES OF ETERNITY

The sun is drowning
Down beneath the sea it goes
The sky is pink and orange
It's a perfect picture

The waves with snowy ends
Come crashing against the cliffs
They climb as high as the sky
Then come crashing down

Only to come again and again
Their energy never wanes
Will they ever tire?
Eternal seas of power.

Jenny Pugh (14)
Thomas Telford School, Telford

AUTUMN

Red and gold leaves put altogether,
Every step one more crunch.
You feel the cold wind brushing through your hair,
Trees are bare and so are the streets.
You can smell the autumn dew
And feel the chill in the air
As the sun rises in its autumn gold
And the town wakes up with a sudden yarn.
People gather in the street,
Workman sweeps away the carpet of leaves,
Children all smart for their new school,
Kicking leaves as they fall in their path.

Christopher Airey (11)
Thomas Telford School, Telford

MY CHILDHOOD

Quickly, quickly we have to go
Before the baby starts to show
Dad rushing around
Can't keep his feet on the ground
Dressed quickly in school togs
What about the dog?
Breakfast at our friends
I wonder what we've got?
Cornflakes or toast with an egg on top
Time for school with friends we go
I wonder if the baby has started to show?
At last school has come to an end
Down the street and round the bend
We met Dad on the drive
Your sister has finally arrived.

Stewart Murray (13)
Thomas Telford School, Telford

MY AUTUMN POEM

I get out of bed and feel the freezing cold.
See the children in their costumes running about.
I can smell fresh air and the smoke off fireworks,
All around me.
Red and yellow leaves scattered across the floor.
I go back into my bedroom and I can feel the cold.
The trees are bare and the church bells are ringing.
Children are walking quickly to get to their first day at school.
But suddenly it changes to winter, it went so fast.
October will be back though, for Hallowe'en and Bonfire Night.

Hannah Abbiss (11)
Thomas Telford School, Telford

Jumpers For Goalposts

Do you want to come and have a game with the lads?
All you need is a pair of shin pads.
Just bring some trainers and the rest,
You don't have to be the very best.

We're just going down the park,
Never know, you could be the next Alan Clarke.
OK, ready, we've got kick,
Watch that boy, he's the best of the pick.

I have the ball; I pass it over there
To that boy who doesn't share.
He crosses the ball into the box,
That boy scores, the one who always pulls up his socks.

The final score, 2-1 to us,
While all the others make a fuss.
My mom pulls up in the car,
'Did you have a nice time?'
'Yes Ma.'

Bobby Russell (11)
Thomas Telford School, Telford

The Elephant

The elephant wobbles
From side to side,
Taking really really
Huge strides.

He trudges on,
Pain unbearable,
He grunts in pain,
Ignores the animals staring.

He can't go on,
Down he went,
Fallen to the floor,
His life money spent.

Sophie Boden (11)
Thomas Telford School, Telford

THE EARTH'S RICHES

Pollution and war destroying this wonderful Earth,
Evaporating all its goodness and worth.
Grass, trees and flowers,
Processed with Mother Nature's powers.
Even though some parts of the world are cared for,
There are some countries which need more.
War ending lives, separating families,
Husbands and wives.
Clean water is one thing they need,
'My children are dying because of this liquid, please help us,'
they plead.

The Twin Towers that crashed to the ground,
People obeyed their leader, who has never been found.
Earthquakes shatter lives and dreams,
Destroying towns and cities that used to gleam.
Rain gushing into houses forming a flood,
No use using your hood!
The ozone layer that stops us from frying,
Has holes in it and like us, is crying.
These are only some of life's ditches
And writing this poem has made me think about the Earth's riches.

Catherine Rogers (11)
Thomas Telford School, Telford

HERCULES

The roaring noise echoes in my ears,
The constant balling thunder of the engines increases my fear.
Endless streams of clouds fly by,
Myself, I feel motionless.
Down below, the fields, they run deep and green,
Millions of dots scattered all over the shot,
Visions of school war videos passing my mind.
Do I have the courage to do it?
Can I devastate this community?

The thunder still echoing, the clouds still moving, the ground lies still.
Time seems to have froze.
The feeling, it's like one of those when you are on a large theme park
Ride, which haunts you at the top before the drop.
I'm not sure if I can press release, all those innocents, all those children,
All those people.

Flames, roars, explosions,
A mushroom cloud fills the air.
Dreams are ended.

Alex Humphries (15)
Thomas Telford School, Telford

AUTUMN

Leaves are turning from green to red
Covering the pavement in a multicoloured bed.
Conkers delight children, big and small
Anxiously waiting for them to fall.

Animals looking for somewhere to doze,
Whilst robins await the winter snows.
Birds flying off to a warmer home,
Hopefully they're not alone!

The creeping frost makes us shiver,
Freezing up the swollen river.
Spilling over the icy weir
Autumn has gone, winter is here.

Neil Allard (11)
Thomas Telford School, Telford

STARS

A midnight sky lies full of stars,
A black velvet cushion covered in glistening diamonds,
Each star is significant,
Or is it?
Does one star shine brighter than any other?
One bright star may catch your eye,
But how long until another comes along?
Each night that star may wait for you,
It may know what you are thinking or how you feel,
It may be who you talk to in the dead of the night.
During the day you may not be able to see it,
But deep down you know that it is there,
Or is it?
Through the troubled times in the day you may not know where to go,
But along comes the night and everything goes into place again,
Until the next time,
Or does it?
Remember, in the difficult times and in the better,
There will be a shining star in the sky for you.

Kim Shepherd (13)
Thomas Telford School, Telford

UNWANTED VISITOR

On a dark, cold night,
there was a man, ready to put
up a fight;
for a piece of *gold,*
or something valuable and old.
He strikes when you're asleep or out
and when you get back you'll know
he's been about.
He doesn't care for you or me,
as long as he gets enough to make
himself happy;
he gets through a door
and then crawls on the floor.
A very clever man is he
and he certainly doesn't come for
a cup of tea.
On a dark, cold night
there was a man, ready
to put up a fight.

Ben Hamilton (11)
Thomas Telford School, Telford

A SUN!

A sun is hot!
A sun is summer!
A sun is reddy-orange!
A sun is a blaze of fire!
A sun is love!
A sun is a hot rose!

Kayley Wolfe (12)
Thomas Telford School, Telford

ROAD TO HELL

Dawn had broken but the sun was smeared by the smouldering cloud,
I sat and watched as men around me stirred for combat,
Their faces gaunt from sheer fear,
The ice-cold water had shrivelled my withering feet,
I was in a daze blinkered to the light,
That minuscule light at the end of the long dark tunnel,
I had to pull myself through, men were shouting,
But shouting through fear,
The days of laughter and jeering were now a distant memory,
The weak had fallen at the first hurdle,
The strong were beginning to fade
Bang!
That fearful sound had once again sounded, another one dead,
Or maybe two or three.
Pull yourself together, are you a man or a mouse?
Away I went over the top, that fearful, dreaded disaster area,
Bang!

Tom Pennington (15)
Thomas Telford School, Telford

SNAKE

A snake is green and scaly
He is the season autumn
In a hot sandy desert
He is the hissing wind
He is a green sock
He is a long single bed
He is the Steve Irwin show
He is a piece of long, stringy spaghetti.

Robert Eacock (11)
Thomas Telford School, Telford

MY DOG MILLIE

We got our dog in November
It was a day to remember
We didn't travel far
But she was sick in the car.

My dog Millie
Is a bit silly.

She sleeps on the chair
Which is not very fair
She plays with her toys
And eats all the shoes.

My dog Millie
Is a bit silly.

She only whines
When the doorbell chimes
Then she goes mad
When she sees her dad.

My dog Millie
Is a bit silly.

She likes her treats
And licks her feet
She is my sister
And I would miss her.

My dog Millie.

James Hayes (11)
Thomas Telford School, Telford

MY FIRST DAY

My first day at school was a disaster
I tripped over the headmaster.

Technology is really cool
We used a strange tool
We played with a circuit board
But we didn't end up in a casualty ward
We used a soldering iron
I worked with my friend Brian
We used a battery
But not a PCB
I cut myself with the wire
Because I didn't use the plier
After the teacher told off Kirk
We started doing the practical work.

Science is really cool
It's by the swimming pool
We used a Bunsen burner
But I'm only just a learner
We used an orange flame
I always got the blame
I always loved this super class
I couldn't get the hang of mass
So that is the end of my science rap
So why don't you stand and give me a clap.

So that's the end of the school day
Everything turned out eventually OK!

Thomas Lewis (12)
Thomas Telford School, Telford

THE BEAR

He stands there, tall and strong
On his hind legs where nobody dares to pass.

He lurks there in the dark
Like a match ready to spark.

He waits there for his prey
As groans echo around the cave
To where he waits for his prey.

He's scruffy and brown
Like a thick carpet rug.

He has no time to stand and stare
For family or friends but to be aware.

He waits for hunters gathering
As people come to get his skin.

Leigh Egleton (11)
Thomas Telford School, Telford

WAR

Bent, blind, weary young souls,
Marching to the deafness of falling bombs,
Bloody shoes upon seething skin.
'Another one dead,' they shout,
Two men bearing a stretcher bow to the floor,
A man wearing deep wounds,
Gashes to his legs is picked up like a king.

The large black shiny tubes
With the power to end all life takes part,
But once it has started it is impossible to stop.

Charlotte Clarke (14)
Thomas Telford School, Telford

THE OWL

Its beak is like scissors ready to catch its prey
Its talons are as sharp as needles
And can pierce even the strongest material
So just don't look like food otherwise you're in trouble!

The feathers are as white as snow
Feeling as soft as a blanket
The eyes are as wide as the sun with black olives in the middle
And don't try to run because you won't be able to hear him come
behind you.

If you meet one in the morning it should be asleep
But at night it is out searching for food
It can hear everything around him
Ready to catch its prey.

This is my favourite animal!

Nicholas Cotterill (12)
Thomas Telford School, Telford

MONEY

People, people everywhere,
spending money, no time to spare.
To think that people live on the streets
and eat and drink and sleep in sheets.
If we could spend and save money today,
then we will know these people will be okay.
God made the world so we could die in peace,
not throw each other upon these frosty streets.
So next time you spare some change,
make sure you put it into the charity box,
then we will stick together like solid rocks.

Sukhdeep Sarai (11)
Thomas Telford School, Telford

TRENCH DEATH

Dull grey skies above
A nasty storm on the horizon . . .
More and more go over the top
The face of death on the other side
The ground between draped in bodies
For each man a reminder of his fate
Seas of red on the battlefield
Soldiers of both sides hoping they won't drown in it
No-man's-land in all directions
No escape from danger or death
Every man's face marked with fear and hope
As they get ready to do battle
Will the cruelty never end?

James Whild (15)
Thomas Telford School, Telford

MY HAMSTER, HEATHER

My hamster Heather is fluffy and white,
If you rush up to her you'll give her a fright.
She likes to hang on her cage bars by her feet,
She sleeps all day on her sawdust bed sheet.
She has pink little ears and a pink twitchy nose,
The kitchen for food is where she always goes.
At night she's as busy as a bee,
She loves running around the settee.
She eats and eats and gets very fat,
Last night Dad sat on her and nearly squashed her flat.
She sits in her bowl and eats her food,
When she's in a greedy mood.

Amy Eacock (11)
Thomas Telford School, Telford

1942

As I stood and looked above the shroud I saw
The enemy moving, I saw. What to do? Stand up? Fire? Die?
All were good options. I froze. Not because of the tension.
The temperature froze me through and the floor seemed to be
Freezing up my leg and into my brain. I couldn't think.
They were right in front now.
All of a sudden a deafening blow passed me as the enemy stop
And crawl. Why?
Blood. The person next to me. It's all I saw. Then he wasn't there.

Why so many questions. I thought it would be easy.
Over by Christmas they said. Not likely. It's already 1942.
It was over. Everyone had gone. Nothing left, just a few more craters.
The man next to me had also gone.
On a silver platter to be fed to the ground.
The cold, chilly, arctic ground, in France?
As I stood and looked above the shroud . . . I saw.

Mark Evans (15)
Thomas Telford School, Telford

THE SNOW LEOPARD

The sleek snow leopard,
With fur as soft as a fur coat,
Lives in the depths of the Himalayas,
To survive this dark creature,
Lives on wild sheep and boar,
But soon there will be more sheep and boar,
For the snow leopard shall be no more,
The reason they will be no more,
Is from our selfish doing,
For we humans like to have a creamy soft fur coat!

Kate Harding-Jack (11)
Thomas Telford School, Telford

THE TALL OAK

The seeds were planted and the growth began.
One small split, then another, then another.
Eventually, its roots thrust out into the ground
And it soaks up all it can reach.
A small piece of communication, a chunk of knowledge,
All build up to create the perfect tree.

When it becomes a sapling, it carries on.
Attempting to build up its bank of data,
Until it becomes a talker and a listener,
Understanding others' emotions and feelings,
Helping it to understand itself
And reach its full potential.

Finally, its transformation is complete.
It knows about itself and the world,
Though it never stops reaching out,
Never stops soaking up the facts of life,
Until it becomes the tall, great oak,
Leaving its goodness and richness behind when it's gone.

Sam Harrow (13)
Thomas Telford School, Telford

BLACK MONDAY

Monday morning I am weak
For it's the start of a new week.
A whole week long left to go
Oh boy, oh boy, oh no, oh no.
First lesson slows down and down,
Until all the students wear a frown.

At breakfast we all shout hooray,
For it's the best time of the day.
We get to the line, the café's full,
We sink down and down for the day is dull.
We wait till the dinner line is down,
Eventually we all wipe off our frown.

Abby Clifford (11)
Thomas Telford School, Telford

A SPECIAL GOODBYE

Hearts were torn apart when you left us
How someone could take away the one we loved
I am so confused and full of anger
You will be dearly missed and loved forever

I remember the last time we laughed
The times we had, will never be lost in memories
How I wish I could have said a special goodbye
You will be dearly missed and loved forever

You were so very special to me
No one can ever replace the emptiness in my heart
I hope you are looking down upon us now
You will be dearly missed and loved forever

I know you have gone to a better place
Somewhere quiet, peaceful and full of love
Your place on Earth will never be forgotten
You will be dearly missed and loved forever.

Natasha Young (14)
Thomas Telford School, Telford

ROLLING

Roll, roll,
Nothing can stop me rolling,
My feet just keep on gliding,
Cutting through the air,

Roll, roll,
The wheels like snarling teeth,
Yet supporting my every move,
I feel that I know them,
Like we've been friends for years,
I feel completely capable,
That I can face my fears,

Roll, roll,
My skates are now determined,
They are moulded to my feet,
They won't face down a challenge,
Through my biggest nightmare, I take a leap of faith . . .
I did it, I did it,

Nothing can stop me rolling.

Richard Bramall (13)
Thomas Telford School, Telford

I LOVE FOOTBALL

I love football,
Children I know don't.
When I want to play,
They go grey.

When I see a football,
My toes begin to twitch,
All I want to do
Is kick it on the pitch.

Fiona Jagger (11)
Thomas Telford School, Telford

SUNRISE ROMANCE

His brown eyes sparkled,
His face was bright.
We had walked for miles
Under the starry night.
Hand in hand we walked some more
Along the soft and sandy shore.

The sunrise shone
Across the wild, blue waves
And he looked at me
With his fixing gaze.
He whispered softly in my ear.
What were we really doing here?

He brushed my hair
Out of my face,
I looked across the empty space.
He held me close
With his arm,
His love for me
Made me feel calm.

Emma Stevens (14)
Thomas Telford School, Telford

I WANT TO BE

I want to be a star
And always go far.
I want to be on stage
And never act my age.

I want to be a judge,
But never hold a grudge.
I'd love to wear that wig,
Be bold and really big.

I want to be a teacher,
A class I'd always feature.
An apple a day, perhaps I'd get
If the homework I didn't set.

I want to be a builder
They're big and tall and strong,
Wear scruffy clothes and boots
And work a day that's long.

I want to be a dentist
They're never really liked,
Drilling deep and pulling teeth
Underneath that light.

I want to be a carer
And help those ones in need,
I think I might be good at that
To help feed, clothe and read.

I want to be an astronaut,
Stay up in space all day,
Look at the stars and ride round Mars,
Then come back home to play.

But then again!

Perhaps for now
I think I'll just be me
And stay at school,
Obey the rules and
Learn my ABC . . .

Declan Egerton (11)
Thomas Telford School, Telford

TENERIFE!

Shading palm trees all around,
Tropical music was the only sound.
I lay on my lilo looking up at the sky
And I watch the clouds pass me by.
They look like cotton buds, floating past,
Ever so slowly, not very fast.
So relaxing is floating on the sea,
Nothing really seemed to scare me.
Until,
I dared to move because I was too hot,
I was on a lilo how could I have forgot?
Now in the sea I started to cry
I wish I were home nice and dry.
It wasn't very deep, but I was still scared,
I wouldn't do this even if I were dared!
I tried and tried and in the end I was on,
But I looked up and my parents had gone.
Had they left me here all alone?
Had they gone to town or had they gone home?
I paddled back to shore to find my mum,
But they were at the bar getting a drink of rum!
I sat down, had a drink, looked up at the sky
And watched the clouds pass me by.

Carlene Bates (14)
Thomas Telford School, Telford

PETS

My mum and dad must be mad because we own a zoo!
I have three cats, a rabbit, a dog and loads of fishes too.

The cats are fluffy, furry and cute and jump and play around,
The goldfish are boring, just swim about and never make a sound.

Our dog is called Heidi Hedges and her coat is black and gold,
Her dog hair gets everywhere but stops her getting cold!

Barney the rabbit lives in his hutch sleeping on fresh hay,
My sister Ellie and I go out and feed him twice a day.

The best thing about having pets is that they are always there,
Even when you have had a bad day, you know that they care.

When I get in from school, or wherever else I have been,
The dog likes to attack me with kisses and makes me giggle and scream.

'Naughty dog,' my dad says and chases her outside,
'Never have this trouble with the fish,' says Mum - with a little sigh!

Gemma Hedges (12)
Thomas Telford School, Telford

OUR DOGS

They bark and growl at every noise
They really dislike the paper boys
But we all know that they are all talk
And their favourite treat is going for a walk.

They love to have their tummies rubbed
But don't like bath time when they have to be scrubbed
I like to see them wag their tails
And can always follow their hairy trails.

They join me in the garden when I am playing ball
And try to lick me better when I have had a fall
I wouldn't be without them, not even for a day
I know that they're my best friends, for always - come what may.

They are of course our family pets
And I'm telling you that they're the best
They are not horses, cows or frogs
They're Joe and Prinny, our lovely dogs.

Ben Hadley-Evans (12)
Thomas Telford School, Telford

THE THING

I saw a shadow creeping,
I heard the thing sleeping,
I smelt the smell of horror,
Will I open the door tomorrow?

I could see the claws a-scraping,
I could see the curtains shaking,
I could hear the sound of horror,
Will I open the curtains tomorrow?

I heard the thing a-growling,
I tasted the fear surrounding,
I smelt the smell of horror,
Will I open the cupboard tomorrow?

I walked up to the cupboard,
I ran up to the door,
I skipped up to the curtains and . . .
Woof! My puppy ran out!

Toni Williams (11)
Thomas Telford School, Telford

Playing Netball!

P ositions encourage us to play our best,
L earning skills as we pass,
A rms arched over opposite teams,
Y elling to get into a space,
I mpatient to get moving,
N ever taking my eyes off the ball,
G enerously passing to fellow teammates.

N udging my way through the crowds of players,
E yeing the ball with all my might,
T rying to stay focused,
B alancing on both feet,
A iming to take a shot,
L istening to encouragement from fellow teammates,
L eaning forward ball skimming through the air.

                    Goal!

Charlotte Evans (11)
Thomas Telford School, Telford

Survivors

Searching through the rubble for any trace of survivors,
Midnight has come but hope is not lost.

We could hear the shudder of debris being moved,
The time seemed endless, the disaster long ago.

We continued to search proudly,
Patriotically, for the sake of our country.

Not far away bodies of dead lay waiting . . . waiting,
Those of our friends, companions and colleagues.

Hannah Taylor (13)
Thomas Telford School, Telford

METAPHORICALLY SPEAKING, LITERALLY DEAD

Dead; I am, for I am dead,
For I am trapped in my own head.
Vocal stop, it takes the toll,
The sex, the drugs,
The rock and roll.
The pen runs dry,
The past is past,
The canvas laid to rest at last.
The tears that run from each of eyes,
They smudge the scripture I despise.
The open window shuts the door,
The tangent flowing, more and more.
I see the light,
It is ahead;
But I am trapped in my own head.

Dead; I am, for I am dead
For I am trapped in my own head.
Not a word can read the role;
The black and white
The life and soul.
The days they fly,
The peace at last.
The blankness gone, the word is cast.
The ink that flows from many tries
The ends of loneliness that it ties.
The harsh wind blows and lays the law
The standstill clear, the meat not raw.
It's black and white,
The script is read . . .
But I am trapped in my own head.

Stef Badger (13)
Thomas Telford School, Telford

REMEMBERING 'BLOOD SUNDAY'

Twisting and turning through time,
with no control over my mind.
I try to push it out of my head,
but it's always playing on my mind.

Bullets, blood and bombs, it isn't that simple,
I keep thinking, *why throw myself into this pit of danger,*
like a gladiator in a coliseum?
I could have died that day, no warning
I had always thought of dying of old age in a hospital.
That's leading a simple life, it's more complicated in Ireland.

Life expectancy does not exist where I come from,
One bomb and you could be gone,
You can't be sure of anything!

This one Sunday was a good example,
Shouldn't someone be able to express their opinions in peace?
Apparently not!
Protest peace in Ireland and you will end up in a shroud
or in hospital.
We were just speaking our minds when . . . a banging sound emerged,
Like the beat of a drum!
The crowd were mowed down like trees in a breeze.
A blood fountain, made me shudder like a coward.
I felt trapped like a fly in a spider's web, I couldn't move,
My legs felt like jelly.

A country split down the middle, civil war, it isn't a pretty sight.
First and last experiences of this, but it still lives on in my mind.

I'm always twisting and turning through time,
Trying to get this burden off my mind!

James Fellows (16)
Thomas Telford School, Telford

BEWARE!

Witches and wizards sitting in a tree,
Doing spells like they shouldn't be.
First comes a *poof*,
Then a horse's hoof,
Then comes another witch,
Who's rather aloof!

Dressed in black with pointed noses,
Agile and slick they count your toes,
Smelly breath, with teeth so black,
They like to catch you on your back.

Potions and cauldrons bubbling away,
Mixing and twisting all of the day!
A flick of this and a flick of that,
The concoction is complete with a bat.
My mistake, it could have been a cat!

Flying around on broomsticks they go,
Where have they gone? I don't know!
Have they gone to Asda, to find another treat?
They'll be glad of the rest as they're dead beat.

They scour the sky with their cats in tow,
Bristles and thistles are hanging so low.
Toto, the cat, is having so much fun,
He's glad now as his work is done.

So be careful when you sleep tonight,
Shut your windows very tight.
In will come a witch in your dream,
You will give out such a loud scream!

Emily Evans (11)
Thomas Telford School, Telford

JACK AND THE BAKED BEANSTALK

Jack was a boy who lived with his mum
And most of the time chewed on gum.
Jack set off down the road
And saw a man with a puffed up toad.
'I'll swap it for one baked bean,
It's the best baked bean you've ever seen.'
Jack thought he'd done a wondrous swap,
Until when he got home his mum shouted, 'Stop!'
'Nothing at all, nothing to be seen.'
'I've only got five baked beans.'
She snatched them and gulped them down,
She felt like she'd eaten a crown.
There was a yell, there was a cry,
The kitchen smelt like a pigsty.
Mother was dead on the floor,
Blood was splattered on the door.
Jack felt fine,
Until he started to climb.
There was a castle at the top,
Poor Jack needed to stop.
'Oh! Ow!' cried the poor chick,
As out popped a golden brick.
The chicken saw Jack and squealed as it groomed,
'Fee, fie, foe, fum!' the giant's voice boomed.
The big giant grabbed hold of Jack,
As he dropped his favourite snack.
'Tryin' to steal me gold, eh lad?
Well now I'm gonna get you bad!'
The giant swung poor Jack around
And threw him crash, bang into the ground!
So that's a lesson to be learned,
Never steal what can't be earned.

Daniel Bevington (11)
Thomas Telford School, Telford

TITANIA'S SPEECH

I know a wood where King Oberon will be,
He rests in darkness, where no one can see
The oak trees surround him, so it's all shade,
Not even a peep where the sun's got a blade.
Daffodils and tulips, nowhere to be seen
He's in a place where no one has been.
These fantasies are all part of his dreams,
When it is midnight and the moonlight gleams.
Everything silent - except for Puck
Who's playing wildly amongst grass and trees.
Suddenly the wind starts to catch a breeze
Fluttering butterflies drift straight past
Everything he sees will be the last.

Holly Haywood (11)
Thomas Telford School, Telford

THE WOLF

As grey as the night, it wanders through town,
Its eyes probe the ground.
Looking for scraps,
Or the occasional gang of cats.

Alone, it stops by the butcher's door
Before he even found a boar.
As he moves through the night
He will howl at the first sight of moonlight.

He gently returns to his den,
Only to bring back a hen.
As he watches his wife and cub
He wishes he was at the pub.

Joshua Clarke (12)
Thomas Telford School, Telford

WE'RE ENTITLED TO BE DIFFERENT

Do people laugh and point at you or whisper to their friends?
Well ignore them because it's okay to be different
If we all had the same hair colour or had the most expensive shoes
Life would be boring and you'd be bored of being the same.

We're entitled to our opinion, don't change what you think
Because you want to be the same as your best friend
Would you change your hairstyle or colour to be the same
As everybody else?
Because everybody should be different to suit our opinion.

Your friends may have the best football boots or be
Interested in different hobbies
But you can be different whatever they think
One thing in life is important,
That you're happy each day that you live
Whatever they may think.

Ben Marshall (11)
Thomas Telford School, Telford

HOMEWORK, OH HOMEWORK!

Homework, oh homework!
I really hate you,
I wish I could flush you down the loo.
Homework, oh homework!
I wish you didn't exist,
I feel like punching you with my fist.
Homework, oh homework!
I've got you again,
I'd rather be standing in the rain.

Homework, I really can't cope with you,
I don't think my mom and dad can too.
I'd rather go out and play with my friends,
Instead of doing homework which never ends.
Maths, science, English as well,
There's really so much more I could tell.
Now my homework is almost done,
Maybe homework is sort of fun.

Alex Punter (11)
Thomas Telford School, Telford

AUTUMN

Golden, orange and red leaves,
That crunch and crackle when you step on them,
Children laughing, smiling, full of glee,
As they knock on doors and ask,
'Trick or treat!'
In full Hallowe'en costume,
With pumpkins cut to look like monsters in the night
And candles lit inside, make them forever bright.
The smoky haze that fills the air,
As bonfires burn and fireworks flash
And shower their pretty sparks in the air,
Sparklers sparkle all through the night,
Chestnuts are roasted on the open fire,
When the nights get longer and coolness is in the air,
Warm jackets and gloves are brought out the wardrobe for wear,
As wind blows there is a definite feeling,
That once again autumn is here!

Philip Duffy (11)
Thomas Telford School, Telford

FALLEN ANGEL

Mine eyes doth burn
And each in turn
Searing into my skull.

My tongue is like lead,
Problems gathering inside my head,
My mind a tormented bull.

You seem pleased
At my unease,
A smirk spreading on your face.

Yet each bruise
That you use,
To put me down a pace.

My broken legs, beneath me fall,
My shattered wings don't fly at all.
My halo, long since gone.

You ended me,
With your evil glee,
My life is over, done.

Annie Weston (13)
Thomas Telford School, Telford

FIRE, FIRE

Fire, fire burning bright
Is this the wish for all the night?
When animals scatter and free they run,
Thinking they just see the sun.

Leaping flames surround it tight,
Whilst the orange sparks increase in height.
Crackling woods see lights shine through,
Why, when, where, who?

Aimee Slatcher (11)
Thomas Telford School, Telford

THE GENTLE BREEZE

The gentle breeze,
Rustles leaves,
Whilst flowing through the air.
It picks up scents
And then repents
Those it doesn't enjoy.

Then down it goes,
To a child's nose,
Who is taken by its scent,
The child then follows,
This scent that bellows,
'Follow me to go to Heaven.'

This young child,
Not then knowing,
That Heaven means that you are going,
Going to leave the ones you love,
The ones that care,
Who'll never again notice you there,
But only hear you as a rustle of leaves.

Helene Burrell (11)
Thomas Telford School, Telford

NEW SCHOOL

I leave my house with a face of terror,
This small walk which takes forever.

On the way I see nobody, hear nobody and
Worst of all, know nobody.

I get to school, I'm the only one there,
Is this the right time? Is this the right day?

I was about to cry,
I wanted to run home where I knew I'd be safe.

I checked my bag: pen, pencil and dinner money.
A clap of lightning and the playground is full!

Everyone's smart, everyone's clean,
Everyone's calm, but why not me?

In we marched like in the army; two in a row.
Left! Right! Left! Right! No talking at the back.

At the end of the day.
When are the holidays?

Nick Jones (11)
Thomas Telford School, Telford

THE SEA POEM

The sea is green and blue,
It's lovely to see
I hope you like it too
Just as much as me

I love to paddle in it,
And get my feet all sandy.
And then I go and sit
And eat all my candy.

When I go to collect shells
I put them in a bucket.
I wash them in a well
Start singing and my mom says, 'Shut up!'

Rebekka Evans (11)
Thomas Telford School, Telford

AUTUMN TIME

Autumn's the nicest month of the year
Crunching and crackling you will hear
The laughing of children as they play in the leaves,
Rolling about on their hands and their knees.

Trying to catch the leaves as they fall,
Doesn't matter if you're big or small.
There's a chill in the air, it's beginning to get cold.
Start wearing your gloves and hat, I've been told.

The sun is shining and the trees look their best,
Their leaves aglow with colour, they outdo the rest.
Green, gold, yellow, amber and rust,
Floating slowly to the ground, they won't be rushed.

Squirrels running and jumping a dance,
In and out, up and down they prance.
Collecting food, winter's on its way,
It's getting darker, it's near the end of the day.

Yes, autumn's my favourite time of the year,
The spectacular views, always fill me with cheer.
I'll never ever take what I can see for granted
As I wonder how all those trees got planted.

Claudia Hollins (11)
Thomas Telford School, Telford

Day Out

Off we go to the sea again,
Out of our crowded town.
Leaving our house and pets back home,
It's over the hills and down.
Fathers driving the car for us,
Mothers brought our tea.
We will have a wonderful time,
Playing beside the sea.

The beach is very crowded,
With the sea and sky so blue,
Out comes our swimwear,
Which we brought brand new.
Children building sandcastles,
Others in the sea.
Mom is sunbathing calmly,
Dad is as hot as can be.

Jodie O'Hagan (11)
Thomas Telford School, Telford

The Stray Cat

He sits in the dark, nowhere to go
And nowhere to hide
The horrible hunger inside his stomach
The door shut tight
So he couldn't get get in

He walked away from the door
Drooping eyes and all
He headed towards the woods
Searching for help, or else he would die of starvation

He saw light and ran as fast as he could
To get to the light
But the faster he ran the further it went away
So he just gave up

He heard noises, as the hunters got nearer
He thought help was coming . . .
A gun came into view
Boom! The cat fell to the floor
He was dead.

Adam Carr (13)
Thomas Telford School, Telford

SUN

He smiled at me today,
He beamed at me in a special way.
I see him each day and when I looked he smiled!
He beamed down on me as if I were a newborn child.

He made me feel safe today,
Before he went back hiding away.
He's all around me, in a hug
He's a twinkle in my eye, he makes me feel snug.

He glowed in my eyes,
Taking me by surprise.
I looked away, for him I couldn't face,
But he continued to be full of grace.

I saw him again today, but I see him each day each week,
Does he change? I cannot tell, my eyes do not want to seek.
I must admit he is the most fantastic, dazzling person I know,
He will always be around me, a powerful, brilliant, glistening glow.

Hannah Davie (13)
Thomas Telford School, Telford

AUTUMN

Leaves, leaves everywhere, on the ground, in the air,
Crackling under our feet.
Bare trees, seeming as if they have died,
Their colour drained out of them.
The leaves all brown and crinkled, all over the floor,
Waiting to be swept up.
The sun is shining, but it is not warm,
The cold wind breathing down our necks.
The dark comes quicker and the light later,
The night is cold, but hard and breezy.
We walk down the street, hands in pockets
And coats partly covering our rosy cheeks.
Winter is approaching, car windows ice over during the night,
The air is icy, cold and fresh.
The dead leaves slowly disappear,
Autumn has gone and winter has come.

Will Hemming (11)
Thomas Telford School, Telford

A HALLOWE'EN POEM

It's autumn and Hallowe'en is here
The trick or treaters are near,
The lovely costumes the kids all wear
Just to give the people a scare,
I give them a treat,
A nice little sweet for them to eat,
They're happy as they leave our drive,
It's just as the next group arrive.
As the next group go,
I see all the pumpkins glow.

Nisha Mansurali (11)
Thomas Telford School, Telford

A SINGLE ROSE

On this day, I give to you
A single rose, to help you through,
That terrible day when lives were lost
Three thousand deaths was the cost.

September 11th

We shall remember, those who were brave,
But we're sorry for the lives that we could not save.
The United States are stronger now,
When we are reminded our heads will bow.

September 11th

On this day, I give to you
A special rose, to help you through
That terrible day when lives were lost,
Three thousand deaths was the cost.

Katie Lannie (13)
Thomas Telford School, Telford

LOVE

Love is red and pink
Love tastes like strawberry cream
And smells full of aroma
Love looks like a newborn puppy
It sounds like songbirds singing
It feels like a cuddly teddy bear
Love is beautiful.

Elliott Sterling (11)
Thomas Telford School, Telford

THE NEWBORN

Something's coming, I could feel it,
My mum could,
She had a lump in her tummy,
A big one.

I didn't know what it was,
She wouldn't tell me,
But it was living,
Another heart inside.

There it is,
A child,
A little boy,
A sweet little boy.

His beautiful skin shimmering in the sun,
His eyes sparkling,
Really cute
And my little brother!

Nicola Derry (11)
Thomas Telford School, Telford

TIGER

The tiger prowls softly through the jungle
Making himself look like a king.
His large feet cracking branches as he walks,
Smaller creatures darting out of his path.

Vibrant orange
And big, bold stripes of black
That make him stand out
Strong and sleek.
He brushes past the undergrowth.

Savagely he tears apart his prey,
Ferociously snarling
And carries it back home carefully
To his anxiously waiting family.

His young, princely son
With his soft, fluffy coat,
Snarls with appreciation
And licks his lips,
As the king looks admiringly on.

Amy Brentnall (12)
Thomas Telford School, Telford

FOOTBALL

Football, football,
Football mad
Girls think football's pretty sad,
Kicking that ball
Thinking they're tall,
Scoring goals,
Losing their soles,
No time to mime
Because it's half-time.

Football, football,
That is all,
No time for shopping in the mall.
As they play
The one way,
Score another three,
Then you'll see,
We'll be reigning champions!

Declan Allen (11)
Thomas Telford School, Telford

BEING UNIQUE!

Who's to say you're different?
Why should they decide?
They only look on the outside,
They don't care about the inside.
So maybe you can't keep up or join in with their games,
That only makes you special
After all we're all the same,
If they tease and taunt you
Just take it in your stride
What do they know about being unique?
Just stay clear and stand aside
You are your own person
Be proud and stand up tall
Besides what do they know?
They don't matter at all!

Emma McKee (11)
Thomas Telford School, Telford

MY NEW SCHOOL

My new school is great,
They even wash your plate.
A lot of sports to choose,
Hockey, netball, football we never lose.
We all have great fun
And enjoy playing in the sun.

It's nice I've made new friends,
They're into all the trends.
We chat, laugh and express our views
And listen to all the news.
Wolverhampton, Telford, we come from all over,
We feel proud and lucky, like finding a four-leaf clover.

We are all going to try our best,
Especially in our test.
We all hope for grade As,
But are grateful for good days.
At Thomas Telford School,
Now it has a pool.

Lauren Poole (11)
Thomas Telford School, Telford

PYRAMIDS

Oh pyramids, how mighty you did stand,
Once.
Now you are just another tourist attraction.
Oh, what majestic symbols you did make,
Once.
Now you are but a crumbling ruin.
Oh, on you a thousand hours of toil were spent,
Once.
Now you are just an empty shell of a culture that is no more.
Now.

Piles of gold, treasures untold, were entrusted to you,
Once.
Now you are just another camera flash.
Your walls of stone knew mysteries, secrets and ways of old,
Once.
Now they are taken to pieces, they make nice souvenirs.
Workers once crowded together in admiration, awe-struck,
Once.
Now tacky guidebooks are sold, cheap plastic replicas are bought. *Now.*
And that is the ultimate disrespect, a wound even time cannot heal.

Gemma Conroy (13)
Thomas Telford School, Telford

YESTERDAY

Today.
Is it going to be today?
Is it going to be today that I murder?
Is it going to be today that I'm murdered?
Today is the first day of the rest of our lives.
Tomorrow is too late to pretend that everything's alright.
I'm not getting any younger.

Another turning point,
Another fork stuck in the road.
Time grabs you by the wrist,
Directs you where to go.
So take the photographs and still frames in your mind,
Hang them on a shelf in good health and good time.
Tattoos of memories and asking on trial,
Is it going to be today that I confess my denial?

Daniel Brittle (15)
Thomas Telford School, Telford

UNTITLED

She sits and wonders lonely in a crowd
The noise runs past her, breathing aloud
She is a stranger in her secret place
A loser in life's continuous race

All hope seems lost as she breaks to tears
Then from the crowd a face appears
A rainbow in her darkened eyes
A friend to wash her clean of lies

Smiling glee that child felt
A smile to make the coldest hearts melt
And if tomorrow isn't bright
A friend is there to help her fight.

Amber Strickland (13)
Thomas Telford School, Telford

MOONSHINE

Far and away
the moon shines bright,
afraid to smile
except at night.

Just a face
among a crowd,
the others all
seem strong and proud.

But underneath
their perfect shine,
their hearts beat
the same as mine.

So why should mine
be just a face,
just a face
among a crowd?

And yet, far and away
the moon shines bright.
She's the one,
the one that shines at night.

Natalie Lewis (13)
Thomas Telford School, Telford

MY BEST FRIEND!

Exploring the garden, out with my mum
Lots to do, lots to be done
I was only little and very small
Enjoying the sunshine, which I adore
There she was, small and scraggy
Walking along with her little body
Very weak and very scared
But I was different, I really cared
Mum and Dad phoned, where did she belong?
The police, the kennels - her owners had done her wrong
We gave her a home, she was mine
I named her Chip and gave her time
12 years on and still I care
My best friend and I have many memories to share.

Graham Thwaites (13)
Thomas Telford School, Telford

WINNING!

Winning is a pleasure
That you cannot measure
After coming off the pitch with a smile
You know your effort was all worthwhile

All the crowd, chanting in my ear
All of a sudden I have nothing to fear
Passing the ball in the team
Running along like a train on full steam

I aimed for the goal
And what did I see?
My mum screaming for me,
'He scored, he scored, he scored.'

George Udall (13)
Thomas Telford School, Telford

GHOSTS CAN'T DIE

As the speeding car races over the hill,
The murky trees passing still.
Eternal darkness in every way,
'Slow down, slow down,' I hushingly say.
'No!' replies the cold mad voice,
Harsh and powerful, I had no choice.
The echoing voice of men now lost,
Their rotten bodies lay in the frost.

The trees grow thicker,
The darkness slicker.
Smooth like the skull of ended man,
We will leave this hellhole, if we can.
The car does swerve,
Grows my nerve.
As the car is mangled,
In the wreck I am strangled.

50 years on my ghost still lies,
50 years on my ghost still cries.
Every day I am living in pain,
Every day I try to die, in vain.
Can't move, can't sleep,
Nothing but weep.
'Kill me, kill me!' out loud I cry,
But then I remember, ghosts can't die.

Tom Meaney (13)
Thomas Telford School, Telford

SOMEONE WHO HAS INFLUENCED ME

My auntie Pam
Loves dogs
Takes in strays
Painfully thin
Matted coats
Missing limbs
Old, blind
Who nobody wants
Gives them a home
A place to feel loved.

Always smiles
Walks miles and miles
Goes to the kennels
Three times a week
To help the dogs
She's unable to keep.

Raising funds
With loyal supporters
Most of whom
Are doggie walkers.

I hope that I
Can be like Pam
And help those dogs
Out of a jam.

Ben Jones (13)
Thomas Telford School, Telford

MY NAN

Every day I went to see her
It was like a harpoon hitting my heart,
The anguish of seeing the pain in her eyes,
When I knew all she wanted was to smile.
I wanted to help her, but there was nothing I could do,
Except give her my love and support,
Although I knew it made no difference in the end.

When she had gone it felt as if my body was disintegrating
Into small molecules in a cauldron of flames,
But I had to face it, she was gone from sight,
But not from mind,
Because all the happy memories still live on.

Although I still wish one thing
And that is for her to come back to see me for one last time.

Michael Goodall (13)
Thomas Telford School, Telford

THE WITCH

A witch is black.
She is winter.
In a run-down castle.
She is thunder.
A box of darkness.
The show that was banned.
A stale piece of bread.

Joanne Hart (11)
Thomas Telford School, Telford

THE MAD DOCTOR OF SLATER HOUSE

The doctor lurks in the darkness,
So you don't know where to hide.
He runs faster than leopards
Through streets broad and narrow.

He runs through the towns,
Running faster than air.
He walks through the street
Ready to pounce.

Then the victim turns the corner,
The doctor strikes,
The victim, six foot tall,
Did not stand a chance.

The madman runs back home.
When he gets there,
He ticks off his list
The number, 500, he's killed.

Edward Cooper (11)
Thomas Telford School, Telford

NATURE IS BEAUTIFUL

The tree that grows in the garden,
Surrounded by the jade-green grass.
The buds that open into beautiful flowers,
Next to the pavement where all the feet pass.

The rabbits that play hide-and-seek in their burrows,
Chirping birds soaring through the cloudless sky.
The squirrels that climb up the trees
And the foxes creeping, watching so sly.

The people that watch nature,
The best thing there ever could be.
Wherever you may see it,
Either land or sea.

Bethany Tranter (11)
Thomas Telford School, Telford

WAR?

Trudging pointlessly through the mud,
Boots, torn at the toe,
Bombs dropping, *thud, thud, thud.*
Why must we go to war?

Planes flying in the sky,
Planes bombing
Why oh why?

Terrified wrecks, crawl up the beach,
Machine gun fire overhead,
Victory, seems out of reach.
Why must we go to war?

Medics desperately try to stop the bleedin',
'Scalpel, morphine!' too late, he's dead,
Killed in a moment,
One shot in the head.
Why oh why must we go to war?

Trudging pointlessly through the mud,
Boots, torn at the toe,
Bombs dropping, *thud, thud, thud.*
Why must we go to war?

Paul Herrington (13)
Thomas Telford School, Telford

KICK-OFF

The match kicks off, the ball goes to defence,
The managers are jumping about, 'cause it's really tense.
The ball is at the centre of attack,
'C'mon ref, he's just given our goalie a whack!'
Seven just drove the ball up the wing,
Juggling the ball on his feet, going *ping.*
From a wonderful shot, the net's been shattered,
'C'mon ref, our goalie's just been clattered!'
Ouch! It's a horrible tackle, now he's definitely in the book,
He's made it even worse cos he's given the ref a dirty look.
Goalie pulls off a decent save,
'C'mon ref, he's just put our goalie in his grave!'
Takes the free kick early, but hits the wall,
He boots the ball back, but this time with his all.
Eight, stop pussying about,
'C'mon ref, he's just given our goalie a clout!'
The final whistle is blown, score 4-2,
Oh, what a match we've just been through.

Alex Overton (11)
Thomas Telford School, Telford

THE STORM

It started to snow one winter's day.
I ran upstairs, got dressed and went out to play.
I rolled around in the white, fluffy snow,
I went next door for little Mo.
By the way, this is a boy.
We played outside and giggled with joy.

Kyle Bennett (12)
Thomas Telford School, Telford

FIRST DAY AT THOMAS TELFORD

I woke up and today was the day
I have been dreading and looking forward to,
I got dressed as slow as a tortoise,
My mom waving me goodbye,
On the coach, my heart pounding like a herd of buffalo.

My first lesson was art,
We didn't do much, the teacher only talked.
It was soon breakfast, I wasn't really hungry,
But I had a chocolate croissant.
It was soon time to go to our second lesson.

It was music, it was fun on the keyboards,
Then it was time to go to lunch.
I had chicken burger and chips,
I sat next to my best friend, Ben.

It was time to go to PE,
We had to find out about each other.
We didn't do any football
Because we all forgot our kits.
It was time to go home.

So we got our bags and went off,
I got on the coach and I was so tired.
I could sleep like a rock.

James Dean (11)
Thomas Telford School, Telford

AUTUMN

Toffee apples and Hallowe'en treats,
Getting full from the hot dogs as we eat,
Buying the fruit coming ripe from the trees
And can't wait for candyfloss and doughnut stalls.

Smell the bonfire burning
And the food of a barbecue,
Smell the fireworks as they're blasting off
And the smoke that is left behind.

Watch the leaves as they change colour and flutter in the sky
And see the squirrels collect their nuts and bury them
                                      in their nests up high,
Look at the branches, no leaves there at all,
See people dressing up warm, autumn is here and it's getting cold.

Touch the conkers and tread on the leaves,
Feel the warmth of the bonfire
And feel the cold blowing and messing your hair
And touch the kites that are flying high in the sky.

Hear the bonfire crackling and the fireworks banging in the sky,
The sizzling sparklers leading your way,
As the sun goes down at the end of the day
And listen to the rain clang on the rooftops.

Autumn is here to stay for a while!

Joshua Chadwick (11)
Thomas Telford School, Telford

EMBER

Fiery flame flickers, flashes, flies
Then the wind blows, and then the flame dies

What is left when the flame disappears?
An ember of old of which starts to leer

It flies forward through grass and burns onward ever
A journey unfolds of which it may endeavour

It passes through ice with forth blazing bliss
It passes through water realising a hiss

But when it gets to flame at last it
Burns to ash, falls bit by bit

And makes the fire burn seconds more with hope
To realise an ember to burn and cope.

Thomas Stone (13)
Thomas Telford School, Telford

FARMYARD

Chirping of the birds,
Quacking of the ducks,
Mooing of the cows,
Baaing of the sheep,
Neighing of the horses,
Woofing of the dogs,
Miaowing of the cats,
Chatting of the farmer,
Screaming from the children,
Shouting from the parents,
Noisy place to be.

Emily Carroll (11)
Thomas Telford School, Telford

MY CATS

First there was a cat called Jo,
Only four teeth left, the rest had to go,
In old age he loves to moan,
The laziest cat I've ever known.

Then there was a cat called Ebony,
A little bundle of joy to me,
Always pestering me, wanting to play,
I will keep these memories in my heart to this day.

Next came a kitten called Dylan,
He kills everything he can catch, he's a bit of a villain,
But at heart he loves affection
And offers me his protection.

Last of all it's a cat called Lilly,
When she sees me she's very silly,
Firstly she comes, then turns and runs away,
But I know she really wants to play.

Jessica Ross (11)
Thomas Telford School, Telford

THE ULTIMATE THING

Football is the ultimate thing,
It makes me want to sing.
Every day when I play
It makes me feel happy and gay.

If you support Man Utd,
People will hate you.
You play with a ball,
I'll give you a call.

Football is the ultimate thing,
It makes me want to sing.
Every day when I play,
It makes me feel happy and gay.

Adam Brindley (11)
Thomas Telford School, Telford

FOOTBALL

I love football, it's the best,
I always wear my lucky vest,
I get changed into my strip,
I take good care so the shirt doesn't rip.
I quickly slip on my boots,
My mum always says don't grow roots,
Off we go in the car,
I start to dream of being a superstar.
As we get there the moment's tense,
We try and slither through the fence,
I sprint off to get warmed-up,
I have a gulp from my favourite cup,
We get into our starting places,
My friend forgets to tie his laces.
The whistle is blown and the match kicks off,
I always try not to get sent-off,
The ball is passed to the wing,
I run into the box to give it a ping,
The score has changed, we're one-nil down,
I have lost my golden crown,
Am I a circus clown?

Thomas Brown (11)
Thomas Telford School, Telford

IT'S A CRUEL WORLD

I'm a young boy
With my life ahead of me,
But all I see and hear,
Is death and violence on my TV.

I see children starving
Alone in the street,
Crying for their mothers,
No shoes on their feet.

Bombs and destruction,
In other countries,
Why must this happen?
Could this happen to me?

When night-time comes,
Upstairs I tread,
My parents come later,
Kiss me goodnight in my bed.

I think of the children,
In countries of trouble and strife,
What can we do as a nation
To give them hope and life?

Ayden Smith (11)
Thomas Telford School, Telford

THE WORLD AS WE SEE IT

Big and round,
Green and blue,
24 hour clock,
Day and night,
Dark and light.

Pollution is our plight,
To get the world right,
Factory smoke in the air,
People worry and stare,
We should take more care.

Daniel Podmore (11)
Thomas Telford School, Telford

THE WRITER OF THIS POEM

(Based on 'The Writer of This Poem' by Roger McGough)

The writer of this poem
Is as cunning as a cat,
As cool as a cucumber,
As sneaky as a rat.

As funny as a comedian,
As quick as a lick,
As clumsy as a clown,
As clever as a tick!

As happy as a smiley face,
As sharp as a nib,
As strong as a heavyweight,
As tricky as a fib.

As bold as a boxing glove,
As supple as a snake,
As courageous as a lion,
As sweet as a cake.

The writer of the poem
Never ceases to amaze,
She's one in a million, billion,
(Or so the poem says.)

Leanne Graham (11)
Thomas Telford School, Telford

REKINDLED

I stare blindly at the picture on the wall,
The whitewash of the sea,
My mind wanders inwards
Remembering a far-off shore,
It's blank, white and cold.

The sand is arid and empty,
I feel famished and desperately cold,
To live, I must gather wood
And form that vital spark.

Surroundings are tangled and messy
But there is wood to be found
In the dank and barren midst.
A woodpile forms slowly,
Paper adds to the bulk;
We must ignite to live.

A stick I sharpen to a point,
Rubbing vigorously, the heat builds,
Unclear grey smoke mists my eyes -
The first flicker of a flame appears,
A delicate blow gives gentle haste.

Light and bright colour fills the void,
Heat becomes intense, burning through me,
More paper is needed,
The fire strengthens, enlarges,
Patterns dance in fluid motion,
Beautiful, perfect.

The fire burns, unaware of time
But time must end;
The flames die down but the embers remain
May others find warmth in them.

Chantelle Holt (13)
Thomas Telford School, Telford

BLOCKED WITH CEMENT

I stand up by the fireplace
A pen clutched between my lounging fingers,
As I look at the grate, the last glowing cinders vanish
Foundations frame a bottomless pit.

Suddenly, from the darkness a cold, clammy hand appears,
Slowly followed by a strong muscular arm.
Minutes later a sturdy, clouded figure joins the limb.

He begins to think, words flow, words flow, words flow,
Flowers and birds cooing, swooping and spying surround him.
He stops, and from his back he brings a warm red brick
He lays it on the ground, and begins his work.

Two long, weary hours pass
And still the work has not really begun,
He bends his back and moves his hungry hands
Only resting as his cement dries.

At midday, his hands blistered and his back like an old tree trunk,
The four main walls are nearly done,
His work evolves into a magician's act
Slowly unfolding until
Exclamation mark, the trick is done,
As the days come to an end
So does the man's hope of ever finishing.
Next day he returns to do his deed
At breakfast the chalky smell of cement hits the air
And then, as if by magic, he is done
The old man tired, his engines worn out.

He begins to admire, his head is full
But so is my page.
I look back to the fire - it is still non-glowing,
But I am. I am done.

Kate Clarke (13)
Thomas Telford School, Telford

FLIGHT

A fuelled pen, ready to use ink,
Awaiting permission to write,
At any time of day
Or at any time of night.

There is no call for lift-off,
All on-board, not impressed,
As minute after minute goes by
They wait to be addressed.

Finally it comes, permission to go
Lift-off is happening now,
Steadily, she climbs up high
And to the sun she bows.

Passengers not stirring anymore:
Travelling distances so vast,
As the captain guides the way
At speeds so very fast.

The plane begins to fall
And lands safe and well,
No petrol in the tank,
No passengers to dwell.

It is now getting late,
The idea is done and away,
The pen is laid on the paper,
Waiting for another day.

Patricia Regis (14)
Thomas Telford School, Telford

WINTER PE LESSON

Freezing PE days
Are never fair,
With wind in our ears
And wind in our hair.

Freezing PE days,
'Don't look so forlorn.
Run round the field,
You'll soon get warm!'

Colder than ever,
We run round the track
While Sir snuggles down
In his warm anorak.

Knees knocking together,
We grab our hockey sticks,
We can't hold them properly,
Our hands are red as bricks.

Ball hits our fingers,
But they're already numb.
The wind in our ears
Pounds like a drum.

'Right kids, that's it,'
Says Sir in an hour,
We head for the changing rooms
And the dreaded shower!

Emily Hunt (11)
Thomas Telford School, Telford

THE SHORT LIFE OF A RUBBER

Clunk! I was thrown up and landed with a thump.
We all trembled, hoping that we would be taken out of this
                                        dreaded darkness.
Then the box lid opened and I saw him,
The god that would take us to a better place.
The others called it the classroom.
Wonder! I was taken.

I was rolled out onto a flat, cold, wooden table
As the box was put away,
Then the god took me and stripped my wrapper.
I was not held for a while,
Then I was picked up by a pair of warm, but hard, hands.

And then, ow! I was thrown down and rubbed
And as the pencil marks disappeared,
I looked at my body, it was black as night and half of it had gone.
Snap! I was broken in two . . .
And I was thrown into the darkness once more,
But this time, without my fellow rubbers.

Jonathan Ince (11)
Thomas Telford School, Telford

HEAVEN AND HELL

Up above the sky so high
Lives an angel in the sky,
Floating about day by day,
Watching people as they pray.

Down below the ground so low
Lives a devil under the ground,
Crawling about day by day,
Watching people as they lose their way.

Everything is between the two,
But who decides? It isn't you,
It's God Almighty,
It's true! It's true.

Amy Stevens (11)
Thomas Telford School, Telford

THE BUTTERFLY PRINT

I am enclosed in darkness and ponder
Racking my brain to exhaustion,
Trapped, no way out,
Blank is my mind and page.

I hear a few murmurs, from the outside world
The world so distant, far
I see a tiny shed of light,
Cold, although it is bright.

Getting brighter and wider,
The light stretches out,
Becoming warmer and in focus
Still trapped but with a definite way out.

The light burns brighter, inside the dark,
Bigger, brighter and hotter, until alas,
It bursts right open,
The whole world is in view.

I spread my beautiful wings afar,
My wings, which I had grown,
I flutter to the fluffy clouds above,
My page is printed.

Laura Brown (13)
Thomas Telford School, Telford

MONDAY, MONDAY

Monday is good,
Monday is fine,
As good as gold,
Lucky as nine.

Tuesday is tired,
Tuesday is drowsy,
Like my old trainers,
Tuesday is lousy.

Wednesday is active,
Wednesday is fun,
It ticks me off
When Wednesday is done.

Thursday is tearful
Thursday is sad,
It brings out emotions
And makes me feel bad.

Friday is great,
Friday is brill!
Shall I paint my school uniform?
I think I will!

Lauren Sneddon (11)
Thomas Telford School, Telford

FRIENDS

Friends are always there,
They always try to care.

They always make you laugh,
They show you the right path.

They tell you all their secrets,
Their wrong-doings and regrets.

You couldn't cope without them,
They're the stars of your life.

Jodie Stokes (11)
Thomas Telford School, Telford

COMPUTERS, COMPUTERS, COMPUTERS

Computers, computers, computers,
I don't know where to start.
What in the world is PC Pro,
And how do I use Clip-art?

I thought a ram lived in a field
And a boot was like a shoe.
When your comp starts feeling sick,
What are you meant to do?

The doctors laughed when I called them,
My parents said, 'What's new?'
The cat just stopped and stared
And I don't have a clue!

I was told of a man named Norton
And he was the one to call,
He fixed my computer in 10 secs flat
And even installed a firewall!

So now my computer's all better,
My keyboard and mouse are OK,
So *don't* even think about touching it,
It's cost me enough for one day.

Rachael Burton (14)
Thomas Telford School, Telford

SUNRISE

The empty darkness surrounding me, before me
No light, no sound, nothing,
Then a glimmer of hope in the east.

As the mighty sun arises
Displaying its power to all near, far, everywhere,
In my mind, the clockwork needs this light.

Shadows appearing - long, dark objects on the floor,
Nothing there in the shadows, blank,
But shorter they go, shorter still,
As the circle begins to form.

Higher and higher, more and more
Less and less darkness of shadows on the floor.
Lighter, brighter, till at full mast,
The sun is straight above us.

The light has come,
The day is here,
My work is done,
No sweat, no fear.

Natalie Corfield (13)
Thomas Telford School, Telford

FIRE

Dancing, flickering, burning light,
Going to get you in the night,
Burns so brightly under the moon,
Going to get you, get you soon.

Devastating, daring and always mean,
It's an evil, destroying, eating machine,
An ominous, raging, psychopath,
A ball of blazing, angry wrath.

Orange, yellow also red,
Nothing or no one can stop it spread
Before it, all things will flee
Terrifies you and terrifies me!

Edward McGovern (11)
Thomas Telford School, Telford

THE HUNT

Light creeps into the forest
To the master it is a beautiful sight,
The sun coming through the trees at dawn,
Signalling a world with daylight.

The slave, however, sees the world differently
He does not see beauty at its best,
No the slave he is doing something different,
He is putting all his senses to the test.

The slave barks out loudly
And a brace of pheasants fly away,
Followed by the sound of gunshots,
This is the world for the day.

And this is what the slave loves doing,
It is all the master will ask,
The hunt goes through the forest all day,
It is not such a difficult task.

And the slave will never be hungry,
Nor will his teeth be blunt,
He does not eat the things we do,
He is filled with the thrills of the hunt.

Matthew Broderick (12)
Thomas Telford School, Telford

MY FIRST DAY

My first day was a disaster,
I tripped up the headmaster.
The day outside was freezing coldly,
My sandwich was really mouldy.
The teacher said my work was messy,
I met a girl whose name was Jessie.
She threw me down,
I hit her back and made her frown.
After that I got lost ten times,
In poetry I couldn't find any rhymes.
Finally time to go home,
My parents forgot and that made me moan.
They came to pick me up (5 hours too late)
I couldn't believe it, was this my fate?

Sarah Gibbons (11)
Thomas Telford School, Telford

THE BIGGEST BLABBERMOUTH IN THE UNIVERSE

My friend saw a spaceship,
It beamed him up,
The aliens told him,
That they would take over the Earth,
But he wasn't allowed to tell anyone.

As soon as he got home he phoned everyone,
The police, army, his friends, everyone,
When the alien spaceship came,
It almost fell from the sky,
It flew as fast as it could away.

The next day the alien ship came,
With TV cameras and a trophy for my friend,
The trophy had something engraved on it,
The Biggest Blabbermouth In The Whole Universe!

Clare Donnelly (11)
Thomas Telford School, Telford

THE SNOWMAN

Out of my window I see the snow,
Falling in one perfect layer,
A clean sheet before me.

Slowly footsteps were made
As he ran across the garden laughing,
Snowballs flew out from behind the shed,
Missing him in the early half-light.

One last attempt met its goal,
He started to roll a ball and
It grew until it was finished at last,
Then came another, bigger than the first.

From the house ran a girl,
Carrying the finishing touches in her arms,
Two coal lumps, a carrot and some string,
The details were all there.

How the snow shines and still it falls,
A sheet covered in marks.

Claire Millward (13)
Thomas Telford School, Telford

FISHING FOR INSPIRATION

My page smooth but blank,
The water, blue but calm.
The line hanging but still,
My pen poised in my palm.

I'm ready for a catch,
Ready for a thought,
I stare at the bait,
For the fish that I sought.

I've been here before
And waited so long,
For some magical words,
For my poem or song.

Yet now they are here,
The thoughts flood my head.
I make myself ready,
For the task ahead.

Now it is here!
My catch of the day,
As my poem is finished
And my thoughts drift away.

Michelle Tombs (13)
Thomas Telford School, Telford

CHOCOLATE

Dark brown and shiny,
Smooth and luscious,
Brittle, sweet and crunchy,
The flavourful, superb, most delightful snack ever eaten!

Thomas Davies (11)
Thomas Telford School, Telford

THE SEASIDE

When I woke up
and looked outside,
the sun was shining
and glistening with pride.
The sea was sparkling,
a wonderful view,
a lovely place
for me and you.

We could go out
onto the sand
and build a castle,
made by hand.
Or we could run
into the sea,
but not for long
because of tea.

Our fun day is over
at the sea,
let's come back next year,
just you and me.

Terri-Leigh Finazzi (11)
Thomas Telford School, Telford

RUBBISH

Last night's curry,
Wednesday's mouldy fish,
A nasty old banana skin and green chips in a dish!
The food in here is awful so don't come inside,
Unless you want a really smelly, nasty, old surprise.

Bradley Edwards (12)
Thomas Telford School, Telford

POSSESSED

I tried to make dinner,
    but the cooker broke,
I tried to make a cup of tea,
    but the kettle burnt out,
I tried to do my homework,
    but the dog ate it,
I tried to watch TV,
    but the TV screen smashed,
I tried to go to Grandma's house on my bike,
    but got a puncture,
So I had to walk to Grandma's,
    to get some dinner,
Hope nothing else goes wrong,
    that will teach them to leave me alone,
I'll be back home soon,
    best they rush back before something else happens.

Daniel St John (11)
Thomas Telford School, Telford

MY MOTORBIKE

Slipping, sliding all over the place,
Woah, woah, this bike's got some pace.
This bike is just so cool,
It makes me look anything but a fool,
I really don't know, I don't know how,
I don't know how I'm riding it now.
What a day, I finished first,
What a bike, what a burst.

Alex Williams (11)
Thomas Telford School, Telford

THE FAT CAT

There was a cat, who was so fat,
The fat cat lay on the mat.

The fat cat, one day was dreaming,
Of birds and mice - what is the meaning
Of the fat cat who was dreaming?

The fat cat who dreamt of food,
But when woken, would be in a mood,
The dream was broken, the dream of food.

The fat cat who was always hoping,
Of birds and mice and all things nice,
The fat cat who was always moping.

The fat cat lay in wait,
Wait . . .
Wait . . .

There was a cat who was so fat,
The fat cat lay on the mat.

Laura Leung (11)
Thomas Telford School, Telford

DEPRESSION

Depression is a deep red
It tastes like cold tea
It smells like cold, stale smoke
It looks like a dusty house
It sounds like heavy breathing
It feels like greasy hair.

Sophie Deans (11)
Thomas Telford School, Telford

THE FRUIT TREE

It started life
With a widening ring,
Like a thrown stone's ripples
From the centre of things
It grows each minute
Filling the space
A shoot from nowhere
Taking its place
A hastening growth
From something so small
Feeding each leaf
Before its fall
The fruit tree blossoms
Till its issue is formed
And the space once empty
Is now adorned.

Kat Howell (13)
Thomas Telford School, Telford

HOMEWORK, OH HOMEWORK

Homework, oh homework - please give me a rest
6 o'clock comes and I'm back at my desk
Reading and writing and doing my maths,
I'd rather be hangin' and having some laughs!

Mom says it's vital to get my degree
Work very hard and soon you will see
As and Bs come to those who work hard
But Es and Fs mean a bad report card.

Working and waiting just to get to bed
Numbers and symbols swim around in my head
Maths and English, I can't take it anymore
You have to do homework, cos it's the law!

Jack Dimmack (11)
Thomas Telford School, Telford

MY TROPICAL ISLAND!

When I look out onto my tropical island,
I can see colourful parrots flying in the air like rainbows,
I can hear waves lapping against the shore like a battle,
I can smell milky coconut in the air,
I can feel hot sand under my feet.

When I look onto my tropical island,
I can see the glistening sea flowing with the wind,
I can hear trickling streams falling into the sea,
I can smell strong, briny salt,
I can feel silky flowers, gentle, in the palm of my hand.

When I look out onto my tropical island,
I can see tall palm trees towering over me,
I can hear laughing pirates in the wind,
I can smell fierce, smoky fires around me,
I can feel slippery rocks in the stream like a bar of wet soap.

When I look out onto my tropical island,
I can see sparkling treasure, hidden underground,
I can hear long whispers of the wind,
I can smell sweet pollen in the flowers like beautiful perfume,
I can feel the sun beating down on me with a warm smile.

Rhiannon Newman (11)
Thomas Telford School, Telford

TASMANIAN DEVIL

Tasmanian Devil is my name,
Being naughty is my game,
Twisting and turning I do for fun,
I love keeping people on the run.

I have a sister who moans and groans,
She loves eating flowers when we leave her alone,
She does it for attention it's plain to see,
My prissy sister really does annoy me.

I love to roam around the woods,
Destroying the trees and eating the slugs,
Then I go home for my tea,
Sandwiches and ice cream, yum, yum, yummy.

Daniel Key (11)
Thomas Telford School, Telford

POEM TO A . . .

Here is a poem to a loving carer,
Here is a poem to someone who comforts others,
Here is a poem to someone who always has time to come,
Here is a poem to my:
   Mum!

Here is a poem to the kindest person,
Here is a poem to a loving one,
Here is a poem to someone who is just a bit mad,
Here is a poem to my:
   Dad!

Theo Berkeley (11)
Thomas Telford School, Telford

THE DAY HAS BEGUN

In my hand
The pen is ready to write
Before I fall into a deep sleep
Full of dreams.

I see someone
In the distance
I cannot make out the face
But she is there.

She moves from her space
Closer, closer to me
I can just see the outline,
Of her slight body.

Now in the light
All is clear,
I can see her beautiful face
She is near.

As the light dims
She becomes shy
She knows I can see her
From the corner of my eye.

Her long golden hair
And her perfect face
Disappear back to her space
My page is full.

Laura Staddon (13)
Thomas Telford School, Telford

DAY AND NIGHT

It's just gone dawn,
There's a cold morning chill in the air,
The rose I can see from my window is sealed shut,
Suddenly a glimpse of light,
The birds begin to sing.

The sunny rose opens to the morning glow,
Its petals a beautiful blue,
The darkness has been cleared . . .
The stem like my pen so strong and bold,
The page in front of me still empty,
Yet my head so full!

Soon the head becomes visible,
A beautiful picture develops, but
How can I capture it?
The leaves come into view . . .
The stem no longer visible,

The sun begins to lower, night is drawing near,
I have but only seen what is possible to see
And cannot see what is not - the roots,
All I can see is the soil surrounding and protecting it.

Darkness falls and my head is cleared,
The page is neatly scattered with words,
The rose closes its delicate petals,
Protecting all the beauty inside,
It is done . . .

Kimberley Martin (14)
Thomas Telford School, Telford

LOVE

Love is the colour dark pink
It tastes like Galaxy chocolate,
It smells like sweet incense,
It looks like lots of hearts,
It sounds like violins,
Love feels like a warm fire,
Love fills me with passion.

Holly Gwilliam (11)
Thomas Telford School, Telford

HATE

Hate is black,
It tastes bitter,
It smells like a burnt-out fire,
It looks like a room where you're all alone,
It sounds like sniggering behind your back,
It makes me feel cold inside.

Danielle Barlow-Exton (11)
Thomas Telford School, Telford

LOVE

Love is red,
It tastes like ripe and sweet strawberries,
It looks like a heart,
It sounds like birds singing,
It makes me feel great.

Emma Evans Gilbert (11)
Thomas Telford School, Telford

MY FAMILY

My family is as nutty as can be
My mum looks sweet
But stings like a bumblebee.

Then there's my dad
He's obsessed with his PC
He likes his football
And his TV.

Rachel, my sister
Ruins my room
Never tidying up
Saying, 'I'll do it soon!'

Me
I'm perfect in every way
Always playing netball
Working hard, night and day.

Victoria Cadd (11)
Thomas Telford School, Telford

LOVE

Love is bright red,
Love tastes like strawberries,
Love smells like roses,
It looks like hearts,
It sounds like doves,
It makes you feel joyful.

Daniel Boden (11)
Thomas Telford School, Telford

A SMALL PIECE OF HISTORY

I am here sitting at my desk,
Searching for inspiration
That will give me an insight into why
I see the image coming into view
And the thoughts I had.

The ghastly image of the coldness
The loneliness of the ice
The feeling that you are all alone,
No one to care and no one with whom to speak.

Ghosts drifting across the Arctic floor,
Stranded, frozen cold,
Nowhere to go, my mind is blank
But now I write and now the Arctic turns into fields of green,
The sudden feeling of warmth.

Trees and flowers break through the misty ice and spring arrives
Sunbeams depart the icy clouds, to create a clear sky,
The page fills and more images appear.

And as my mind fills I feel the icy touch and the coldness
Melting away; and sunbeams making my cold heart grow warm
And as my eyes droop, I see one last image of my beautiful
Spring, as winter drops away.

And now the page is filled, the white Arctic is no more
And now my work is done.

David Adams (14)
Thomas Telford School, Telford

A Sweet, Young Bud

A sweet, young bud,
A quiet little fruit
Sits quivering . . . wavering
In the dark, cloudy bush.

A sweet, young bud
On a still, silent stem;
No scent of a dream, nor sight of notion is found
In the dark, cloudy bush.

A sweet, young flower.
Dewdrops of light fall here and there;
Here and there,
Off the blurred, silent thought.

A sweet, sweet rose,
Fragrant with the freshness of morning.
Pink petals,
Outlined with yellow youth
A green stem quakes over a white sky.

Pricked fingers by a thorny pen
As the sweet, sweet rose's life
Is broken away piece by piece . . .
Petals; leaves;
Just a delicate essence drifts on the breeze.

Kirsty Prince (14)
Thomas Telford School, Telford

MY WINTER VISION

In my winter vision, I see the frozen, sparkling snow particles
falling through the misty, spiral-like fog.

In my winter vision, I see the icy water from the bare, leafless trees
dripping ever so gracefully, one by one onto the vortex-patterned path
that confuses you mentally and physically.

In my winter vision, I can see the diamond-like icicles on the
gargantuan, sight-satisfying cliffs that reach higher than the eagles fly.

In my winter vision, I feel the cool breeze blowing through my hair,
it feels almost like you've dived off the highest mountain
into a cool, peaceful sea.

In my winter vision, I smell . . .
Hang on, you've seen my winter vision, now I want to see yours.

Sarah Jones (11)
Thomas Telford School, Telford

MYSELF

To my parents I am sweet
To my sisters I am a good gymnast
To my friends I am neat
To my grandparents I am very nippy and fast
To my neighbours I am a great fan of meat
To my teachers I am never last
To myself I am well just plain old me!

Katy Louise Foster (11)
Thomas Telford School, Telford

BACK IN THE OLD DAYS

I slipped and fell down
Down in my imagination
I searched for thoughts
A small inspiration
I thought of the happiness, the times I used to have
But there is nobody around anymore to maybe joke and laugh
The days went by when I did not moan or cry
Back in the old days
I'd jump for joy, have fun with my toys
Back in the old days
But now I'm old I have no friends,
I just have memories
Back in the old days.

Nader Morsy (13)
Thomas Telford School, Telford

THE BIRD

The bird,
So elegant and graceful,
So huge and powerful,
So streamlined and swift,
So fast and small.

Dashing round trees,
Darting through woods,
Dropping at rabbits,
Diving at fish.

The bird.

Patrick Lawrie (11)
Thomas Telford School, Telford

AUTUMN

Summer has gone and autumn has come,
It's time for conkers and brown leaves and the wind,
Summer has gone and autumn has come,
It's time for hats and scarves and cold weather again.

Out on the streets the floor is growing,
As it's covered in a blanket of golden leaves,
A squirrel scampers across the road,
Gathering acorns to prepare, for the winter's cruel cold.

It's growing dark already
And the sun is hiding away,
I'm feeling very sleepy,
Although it's only half-past six.

The heavens have now opened
And it's tipping it down with rain,
Everyone outside is running away, in raincoats and gloves
And hats and scarves and their umbrellas,
To escape from wicked autumn.

I can't wait for summer again,
The warm and sunny days,
Trips out to the seaside
And shorts, T-shirts, caps and bare feet.

So please hurry up autumn,
Don't keep me waiting too long,
Bring me the sun back again,
For sunshiny days to come.

Rachel Lloyd (11)
Thomas Telford School, Telford

THE DESTROYER OF WORLDS

My pen rests casually on my palm,
Waiting for the storm before the calm.

I look through the skylight past what I discern,
Into a dark haven that begins to burn.

A hurried shadow runs past, a burning statue near,
A scream and shout, a cry of other worldly fear

For the first time I am noticed, by a man of red eye,
Fixes me with a deathly gaze, then decides to die.

I see the flames more clearly now as they slowly cease to be,
I follow a blind peddler who has lost the will to see.

I see no eyes, I see no ears, I see no faces at all,
Only gaps on a white sheet, no life, no death, back to reality I fall.

David Willett (13)
Thomas Telford School, Telford

LOVE

Love is the colour of deep red,
It tastes like sweet strawberries,
It smells like red roses,
It looks like a field of scented flowers,
It sounds like a rushing river,
It feels like a cosy, lit fire.

Sheena Perry (11)
Thomas Telford School, Telford

FRIENDSHIP

Friends are always there for you,
Even through thick and thin.
They never leave you out
And always bring you in.

Sometimes we have those stupid rows
And we don't speak for a day,
But in the end I know for sure
We'll make up anyway.

Friends are always loving
And always have time to play,
They always keep you company,
Hopefully, every day.

Roopindar Sidhu (12)
Thomas Telford School, Telford

FOOTBALL

Football is my favourite game,
For some who play, the road to fame.

But for me it's just great fun,
Time to play with mates in the sun.

I play right wing for Tetterhall Wood,
Hopefully school striker, if I could.

My top team is Man United,
When I watch them I get so excited.

In the future, perhaps an England star,
But in my dreams would that be too far?

Samuel Rogers (11)
Thomas Telford School, Telford

ON THE BEACH

Look at the sun, how it shines bright,
It gives the Earth warmth and light.
Children are messing about in the sand,
Here comes a seagull about to land.

The sea is rough and the waves are bashing
Against the rock, a sound of clashing.
Seagulls swoop over the beach,
Stealing things within their reach.

Driftwood and shells lie scattered around,
The treasures of the deep wait to be found,
Sandcastles rise, majestic and tall,
The tide comes in and soon they will fall.

William Maiden (11)
Thomas Telford School, Telford

MY POEM

Flying cars, brand new sports,
Walking models in funny shorts,
Parrots swimming, whales flying,
In this world no one should be crying.

Robots doing your homework and also making your beds,
Funny looking people who strangely have 2 heads,
The most noticeable thing of all, are the lilac seas,
Something else that's obvious, are the mooing bees.

No more florescent man-eating plants,
No more wearing your granny's pants,
What on earth will become of me?
Or more important my family!

Mark Trow (11)
Thomas Telford School, Telford

MY TIGER

I held the smooth dark pen,
Staring blankly at the white sheet
And waiting for lost images to fill the space.
All to be heard is the constant ticking of the clock.

I wandered to the other side of the desk,
Desperate for inspiration,
My eyes focus on an animal,
A model tiger, perched thoughtlessly
It lies, motionless.

Then it vanishes, I am left in darkness,
A glimmer of light on the horizon,
Silhouettes of unfamiliar figures
Appear then dissolve into the murky blackness.

A dazzling globe of light rises into the sky
Aiding my vision, I see obscure figures
Of wild animals, glowing eyes stare in my direction,
The harsh, flat landscape holds little vegetation.

As the land rapidly becomes more clear,
I see how many animals merge into the dry landscape,
Yet others stand out, the crash of hooves is heard
From a pack of antelope as the tiger chases.

The background slowly fades away
The foreign noises silence and I am left in a hush,
Staring at the toy tiger, positioned as it was before,
I look down at my pen,
I realise the page is filled.

Jamie Leadbetter (13)
Thomas Telford School, Telford

TIGER

A peaceful silence everywhere,
The tip of the pen quivers, motionless
Nothing stirs;
The dark of a cold night closes in.

Not one noise in this seclude, apart from the swishing,
The repetitive swishing of a tail somewhere in the distance.
Rising and falling . . . rising and falling,
Thud, thud, thud onto the ground beating out consistently.

The noise gets faster and clearer
Dark stripes mark the field of orange,
Clear black marks,
Clear black marks of a tiger.

The image becomes clearer, the eyes shining emerald-green,
Like a torch, uncamouflaged,
The long grasses conceal the body and
Only those black stripes are seen.

It moves, the giant figure heaving silently,
Stretching its long nails,
As clear as day, the tiger watches the movements of young prey,
The tail begins to thump out a death chant,
Its pungent breath pumping into the air.

And it pounces, quick as lightning, its aim is perfect,
The full tiger comes into view in all its magnificence and glory,
It captures the prey, it's such an easy death that none could suspect.
Oblivion, it's all over.

The thudding has stopped,
The dark of the night resumes its steady crawl towards day,
The tiger has finished
And the page is done.

Eloisa Rowland (13)
Thomas Telford School, Telford

COLIN MCRAE

He drives at fast speeds down narrow lanes
And relies on one person to direct him,
One mistake and he'll lose control
And end up in the nearby countryside,
Just like me in rallying games.
It is he who has made me drive fast.

The crashes he has
Are nearly life-threatening
And I've had my fair share of crashes in rallying games,
But it's not the same as in real life,
But after them he acts as if nothing has happened,
As if he doesn't have a care in the world.
If that happened to me,
Flipped upside down and inside out,
In a car at 100mph,
I might be a bit wary next time I got in a car,
But he doesn't seem to have a care,
He just carries on.

He has his fair share of wins and losses,
Last day disasters,
Must make him really disappointed,
But if I lose on a rally game I have the choice to restart it,
But he doesn't have that choice,
He just has to get on with his job.

I wish I could do his job,
But would need to find someone I could trust,
Someone who I could read out warnings at 100mph,
The person who has influenced me is Colin McRae.

Nicholas Turner (13)
Thomas Telford School, Telford

SUNLIGHT

I shone upon a man today
And made him sing and smile,
I warmed the hearts of families
And friends for a while.
I also saw some flowers
And touched them with my glow
I watched them reach towards me
And I laughed as I saw them grow.
I wiped the tears from a girl,
I made her feel some hope
And I made the birds fly and tweet,
I helped people to cope.
But I also stole some water
From the mouths of the weak
I burned the skin off people's backs
And made plants wither and bleak.
I set some grass on fire
And watched the colour spread,
I made the air burn people's lungs
And blacken where creatures tread.
I can be fine and pleasing
Or raging mad and hot,
But nothing can make me weak,
That's something I am not.
Until . . . I tire of shining
And retreat into a cloud
To rest for another night
And let the moon bound.

Samantha Yates (16)
Whiteheath Pupil Referral Unit, Rowley Regis

FIRE

A small boy made me with twigs and leaves,
The more he lit me the more I breathed.
Before long I was big and bold,
Chasing away all of the cold.

The more I burn the bigger I get,
Now the boy's head is full of regret.
He tries to turn and run away
But instead he falls and gets in my way.

He rolls around and screams with pain
As he is covered by my orange flame.
Suddenly his life flashes before him;
He regrets arguing with his mother this morning.

But now it's too late, he has made his mistakes,
His lifeless body lies on the floor,
He won't be able to light me . . .
Anymore.

Faye Sweeney (15)
Whiteheath Pupil Referral Unit, Rowley Regis

FROST

I can freeze water with a single touch,
I can lay frost on the ground with the palm of my hand,
I can make you shiver with one little look,
I make a tree look beautiful with a stroke of my hand,
I make a pond freeze over with a wink and a smile,
I made a road sparkle with ice as I strolled slowly past,
I ran away when I saw the sun come out to play.

Carol Fowkes (15)
Whiteheath Pupil Referral Unit, Rowley Regis

FIRE

I am as bright as a star,
As deadly as poison and as hot as Hell.
I am fire.
I love to spread my arms
Grabbing everything in sight.
I am sometimes good, helping things to keep warm.
I am sometimes bad, hurting trees and homes.
I am just a little child who is as old as the Earth.
I am fire.

Tiffany Talbot (15)
Whiteheath Pupil Referral Unit, Rowley Regis

DESPAIR

I strike without warning
I pierce your heart
I am never welcome yet I always get in
I make the strongest man weak
And the wisest man humble
Nothing can quench me but hope and joy
And then I don't die
I linger on, hiding in the deep recesses of your heart
Waiting to return.

Jordan Oldbury (15)
Whiteheath Pupil Referral Unit, Rowley Regis

WRITING, WRITING

Writing, writing, it's so exciting,
Drawing, drawing, it's so not boring,
Pens and pencils and coloured stencils,
Rubbers, sharpeners all from partners.

Paper clips, folders and plaster of Paris moulders,
Paints and glue, stop you feeling blue,
Staples, rulers and Tipp-Ex for droolers,
Windsor, Windsor, is the best!

Jenny Powell (12)
Windsor High School, Halesowen

FIRE

The rippling, roaring noise it makes,
It's red, yellow and orange all mixed into one.
In my house the fire shakes,
But when water's near it's vanished, it's gone.

The way the flame dances in the dark,
It can be caused by the smallest of sparks,
But once fire starts it gets larger and grows,
The beauty of fire always shows.

Some say it's a spirit, that it has a mind of its own,
But it's linked to the Devil, that's what pictures have shown,
Perhaps it's a murderer in disguise,
But it's so vast, it has nothing to hide.

But why is fire all around
And when will the flames end?
Maybe it comes from the ground,
All I know is, it's not water's friend.

The spell it creates over the human eye,
If you stay with fire too long though, you're certain to die,
So beware of the beast called fire,
Because once it begins it can only get higher.

Claire Elliott (13)
Windsor High School, Halesowen

ROLLER COASTER POEM

As I stood in the queue
I heard somebody say
This ride's pretty daunting
Do you think you'll be okay?

I looked up at the skyline
And there the beast stood
200 feet high
Made from steel not wood

Getting into the giant
My teeth started to rattle
From then on the ride
Was an uphill battle

We'd now left the station
There'd be no turning back
All that lay ahead of me
Was that winding red track

The time had come
I was at the first drop
Now all I wanted
Was for the coaster to stop

I took a deep breath
And closed my eyes tight
I listened to the screams
Of people overwhelmed with fright

Still it continued
Would we ever stop?
Down again we went
My head was gonna pop

Whoosh around the corner
Up the steel track
For I'd no control of anything
I knew there was no way back

I thought it was safe
The end was now near
But still the constant screaming
Was all I could hear

Screech went the brakes
Now I could relax
I had achieved my goal
To ride the Pepsi Max.

Stephen Harrop (14)
Windsor High School, Halesowen

EMOTIONS INSIDE

E   veryone shows emotions
M   ost people smile or cry
O   r pull a frown, jump with joy or punch the air up high
T   imes we show emotions and just don't know why
I   n our hearts we may see
O   ther people's thoughts or dreams
N   obody will ever realise though
S   omebody makes your face glow

I   nside there are many thoughts
N   ot one is forgotten about
S   ome people make you scream, some shout
I   nside there are feelings, hidden away
D   iscovered by friends or family
E   very day in some special way.

Layla Sargent (13)
Windsor High School, Halesowen

THE WRITE STUFF

Even since the beginning of time,
People had to read and write,
So English was started,
And so the Egyptians began,
With various numerals and pictures,
So an alphabet was created.
And when the Romans conquered,
Latin was Europe's tongue,
Except for the far cold north,
But when money ran dry,
They left and Saxons came.
But after Harold Godwinson,
And the famous arrow in his eye,
Normans created the modern tongue,
From the north of France,
Came a new English language.
Later on in life,
The Tudors came to rule,
The most famous writer was born,
A person who has been in all the tests,
With Scottish terror and Italian romance.
Novels, plays, poems and literature,
Are all parts of English,
It will last till the end of time,
Reign of terror on poor innocent pupils,
All over the world.

John Hywel Maxted (13)
Windsor High School, Halesowen

THE THING

It comes to us all
Why do we run?
Why do we try and hide?

All the things we see every day
Remind us of
The thing that comes to us all

When it comes
We stop and stare
We don't even ask why

All we know
Is that the thing inside
Is telling us not to worry

We all do this thing
Some of us expect it
But none of us want it to come

We want it to go away
And disappear
And pretend it never was

I personally am not afraid of this thing
I know it always comes
One day it will come for you

Can you guess what it is?

Shaun Brookes (13)
Windsor High School, Halesowen

WINTER

Winter is cold,
Winter is grey,
The time of year
When night is longer than day.

Winter is dull,
Winter is lonely,
For some it's sad,
For others it's homely.

Winter is a warm time,
Winter is a loving time,
Definitely at Christmas time,
Winter is a wonderful time.

Chris Cole (13)
Windsor High School, Halesowen

THE WRITE STUFF

The write stuff to do is to help other people,
The write stuff to do is not to take drugs,
The write stuff to do is to try hard all your life,
The write stuff to do is work hard all your life,
The write stuff to do is achieve all your goals,
The write stuff to do is forgive and forget,
The write stuff to do is be loyal to your friends,
The write stuff to do is be loyal to yourself.

Louise Cooper (13)
Windsor High School, Halesowen

AUTUMN IS HERE

A   utumn is here
U   nderneath the tree I stand
T   he leaves float down on me
U   nderneath the tree I stand
M   y eyes look around and see
N   o motion like there used to be

I   s autumn here so soon?
S   lowly I walk around

H   ello autumn, you are here
E   very tree will soon be bare
R   ed and brown leaves cover the ground
E   very bird sings its sound.

Louise Siviter (13)
Windsor High School, Halesowen

THE RIGHT STUFF

Some people think the right stuff is drugs
Some people think it's love
The right stuff is what comes from the heart
Words that are said and really are felt
I think the right stuff is feelings
Feelings of the heart, felt deep down inside
Drugs are an illusion, love is a dream
The right stuff is caring so much
It hurts to say goodbye
Right means good stuff, means things,
Good things are felt but not always said
That's not right, say how you feel
And live your dream!

Vicki Blake (13)
Windsor High School, Halesowen

THE RIGHT STUFF

What is right and what is wrong?
When is it singing and when is it song?
Thin and pretty,
Tough and witty.
Is this what we all need to be?

What is fashionable and what is not?
When is it warm and when is it hot?
Confident and loud,
Fitting in with the crowd.
Is this really what people want to see?

What is good and what is bad?
When are you happy and when are you sad?
Compliant yet forceful
Bitchy, unremorseful.
Is this what they want me to be?

What is surrender and what is retreat?
When is it sugary and when is it sweet?
Impolite and rude,
Permanently in a bad mood.
That's what other people see.

What is right and what is wrong?
When is it singing and when is it song?
Quiet and shy,
Thoughtful, not sly.
I'm happier being me.

Lisa Cooper (15)
Windsor High School, Halesowen

GRANDPARENTS

My grandparents are never far apart,
You can't have one without the other,
Not too far away.
Nan and Grandad,
Grandad and my nan.
What love there is in that house.
What warmth in their arms.

My grandparents are very close,
They're always there,
Together.
Always near through troubled times.
Gran and Grandpa,
Grandpa and my gran.
What joy I find in their smiles
There's strange safety in a kiss.

That is what I miss,
A loving house,
Warming hug,
Joyful smile,
Safe kiss.

This has not gone
It is still there.
Only it is not shared
There's only one,

It's Grandad who I miss.

Kimberly Brown (13)
Windsor High School, Halesowen

THE BIG MATCH

The clock strikes two and the tension's building.
Everyone is arriving and the atmosphere is shaping up.
Who will start? Who will win?
These are the decisive questions asked.

Then the clock strikes three and the tension's built high.
The music starts and the team is announced.
Roberts is starting, but will he score?
These are the questions discussed by each and every fan.

The teams emerge, the atmosphere is electric.
A sea of blue and white is all you can see around.
The roar of the fans, the cheers, shouts and screams are heartfelt.
But the final result is on everyone's mind.

Will the long walk home be a victorious one
Or will it be as miserable and dreadful as the weather on this drab
And bitter Saturday afternoon?
As the match kicks off, the determination of these die-hard fans
Is mirrored on the faces of the players.
Will their efforts be enough?
All these questions will be answered
At a quarter to five.
The fans pray, but will their prayers be answered?

Matthew Waterhouse (13)
Windsor High School, Halesowen

OUR TEAM

Our team is so great
Our players are filled with fame.
Our team is a colossal team,
If they do something wrong,
They get the blame.

Next week is the Cup Final.
We have an advantage playing at home.
Our fans fill every seat.
With a tremendous roar
Our players they greet.

Amandeep Singh Mann (14)
Windsor High School, Halesowen

THE RIGHT STUFF

To be the person you dreamed
You need to look inside your soul
Don't let the world bring you down
Just be inspirational

You need self-esteem to survive
Work is your job not your life
Believe in and respect yourself
Beauty comes from within

Nothing eve as bad as it seems
Trust in your heart and you'll achieve anything
Liking yourself is the biggest hurdle
Overcome that and let yourself shine

Sometimes actions speak louder than words
Have strength and bravery, let your voice be heard
As long as you have confidence and a smile
You'll go far in peace

Never be afraid of hard work
Live for the moment, take each day as it comes
Do what you feel, don't give up the fight
Feel good about yourself and you'll enjoy life.

Alexandra Cook (15)
Windsor High School, Halesowen

LONELY!

Sitting there all by yourself
Wishing for someone to appear
You seem to be the only one around
You don't know what to do
Wandering round the street
Sitting on your own is lonely
Being the one and only
Person here to stand
I've never felt so lonely
I'll never understand
Where everyone was and why I wasn't there
Loneliness is everywhere
I see a shadow appearing
I stop to stare, I approach slowly
And still no one is there
I'm still lonely.

Gemma Southall (13)
Windsor High School, Halesowen

FRIENDS

Friends are there to help you
They're there to have a laugh
There are good friends
Bad friends
And some are just plain daft

They take you through the good times
They take you through the bad
They try ever so hard
To make you rather glad

There are times you have a fall out
But not for very long
'Cause there's something in a friendship
That keeps it growing strong.

Jessica Male (13)
Windsor High School, Halesowen

THE RIGHT STUFF ABOUT SCHOOL!

The right subject at the right time,
At the right place,
With the right teacher,
In the right class,
Write in the right books,
With the right pens,
Use the right equipment,
Do the right experiments,
At the right time,
At the right place.

The right place,
The right time,
The right equipment,
The right desk,
The right books,
The right class,
With the right teacher,
Write at the right time,
Write in the right place,
Write here, write now.

Hamzah Ghaleb & Nathan Rowes (12)
Windsor High School, Halesowen

WRITE STUFF

W riting a poem is a fun thing to do, it takes lots of time,
   but it is worth it too.
R ight is my writing hand, the hand I write with best.
   If I didn't have my writing hand I wouldn't do my best.
I like writing, it's exciting, I write about anything
   as long as it's funny.
T aking time to do my best is rewarding,
   but sometimes it can be a bit boring.
E xciting is the word used for writing, it takes lots of time,
   but all the ideas are mine.

S tationery is the thing we write with,
   it comes in lots of shapes and many sizes.
T ens, twenties, thirties, forties are the packs pens comes in,
   before they go in the bin.
U nbelievable colours can be used for all the pictures I have drawn.
F elt tips are a type of colouring crayon, if you have one
   you have to buy them all.
F ancy writing takes a lot of time, but is worth it in the end.

Dominique Hall (12)
Windsor High School, Halesowen

WRITE STUFF

There was once a lonely old cook,
Who wanted to write a book,
So he sat down to write,
With all of his might,
But on the third page he got stuck.

This same old lonely cook,
Continued on writing his book,
But then he got stuck
And ripped up his book,
That silly old lonely cook.

Andrew Powell (12)
Windsor High School, Halesowen

A PHILOSOPHY ON FORGETFULNESS

Sometimes we forget things
And don't want to admit it.
Lying to friends that you've remembered
And not forgotten their tickets.

Forgetting homework's the worst,
It's detention on the double.
Surely teachers forget things sometimes
And they don't get into trouble.

Saying, 'Happy birthday,'
Is better than, 'Sorry, I forgot.
The piece of my brain that remembered
Turned into an empty slot.'

Yes, sometimes we forget things
And boy, don't we regret it!
Just take my advice and always remember . . .
Bother, I've forgotten!

Jennifer Mitchell (11)
Windsor High School, Halesowen

WRITING

When you write
You pick up a pen
You could write about night
Or you could
Write about a fight
Thoughts whirling about
In your head
Thoughts about
What people said
You put your pen to the paper
Make a mark
You've already
Made a start
Your brain is thinking
Your hand
Is *writing*
Life is ticking
And the pen is flicking.

Daniel Rickward (11)
Windsor High School, Halesowen

THE WRITE STUFF

It's 3.30pm and the pencil case is closed,
The child who owns it has packed up and gone home,
When the room door is finally locked,
Silence . . . then the case is rocked!

Two minutes later the zip is removed,
The scared pencils are slowly soothed,
Next the stationery jumps out of the drawer
And using paper lands safe on the floor.

Using erasers they bounce about,
Then approach the door full of doubt,
For the last time they approached this task,
There was a shaky voice and then a gasp!

Deciding not to, they go back home,
Where they enjoy a feast of ice cream cone,
Hours later they sense a rising sun
And a day of being used has just begun!

Emma Pardoe (12)
Windsor High School, Halesowen

THE RIGHT FRIENDS

Abby, Becky and Laura P
Are just the right friends for me.

When we giggle we can't stop
I remember the last time, almost popped.

At sleepovers we watch movies all night long
We sing and dance to our favourite songs.

When we talk we tell each other secrets
Don't tell a soul, we keep it.

In lessons we write notes to each other
If the teacher finds out we're in bother.

When we're in trouble, get a detention
This to our mom's we never mention.

The teacher writes home a letter -
Don't want to do the detention, so we behave better.

Zoe L Shilvock (12)
Windsor High School, Halesowen

THE RIDE

One day I went to the fair,
But my sister didn't seem to care.
We took plenty of money to spend on the rides,
We also brought some guides.

First we went to the fairground,
People bustled all around.
The rides looked exciting,
My nails I was biting,
'Cause the ride by my side looked exhilarating.

We arranged ourselves in the queue line,
As we all read the *Danger* sign.
Then along came the cart,
Like a dart.

As soon as the barriers were bolted shut,
We whizzed down the track with a loud thud,
We were flung to and fro,
As we went high and low,
Then suddenly the ride began to slow.

We shot down the track
And as I looked back,
I saw someone's face
And before I knew it we were back at the base.

The ride was over and finished.

Lauren Matchett (13)
Windsor High School, Halesowen

THE WRITE STUFF!

English lessons. Not always fun
till teacher says, 'Pack up everyone.'
But today was different
and slightly strange
when the teacher said, 'Time for a change.
Get out your things, forget your book
close your eyes and don't look up.
I'll tell you a story, we'll go on a ride
see what adventures you will find.'

We travelled through time, over verbs and nouns
rhyming words and lots of sounds
till we reached a mystical place
with pens and rubbers, a pencil case
without these things I realised
we would not be able to read and write.

These things we take for granted
and never think about
without simple things like rulers and crayons
we'd have nothing to shout about.
No reading of magazines
no writing notes to friends
it's amazing how fun pens can be
in fact it never ends.

Emma Driver (12)
Windsor High School, Halesowen

SUNSET

It was the most beautiful thing that I have ever seen,
It is outside my room in the morning sky,
The morning sky is here, the stars have been,
The sun is rising; the stars will all die,
The brightness of the orange is glaring out,
The blue sky wants to get through but then hides,
The sun chases the clouds about,
The birds are awake and sing with pride,
They flap their wings and joyfully sing,
The sun has now risen to spread out its rays,
The bight blue sky is now appearing,
Soon all the clouds slowly fade away.
As the Earth circles the magical sun,
Another day has already begun.

Nicola Hare (13)
Windsor High School, Halesowen

WRITING MUSIC

The door slams shut,
The pressure's on.
My heart pounding
As I sit down.
The first written notes begin to sound,
As the ivory keys keep pressing down.
I imagine voices humming the tune
And it all comes together to create my tuneful song.

Jackie Hunt (15)
Windsor High School, Halesowen

THE WRITE STUFF

I can write with my left hand
But not very well

I am right-handed
What are you?

Right-handed or left-handed?
I would like to find out

Does writing with your left hand
Make you work harder?

Does writing with your right hand
Make you work faster?

Is it the same
Or is it different?

Please tell me!

David Harrison (13)
Windsor High School, Halesowen

SPECIAL PEN

Pens, pencils, crayons and more,
After a time they are quite a bore,
But right at the bottom there lies one pen,
Keep it, don't lose this pen again,
Even though you've dropped it twice,
Even now it still looks nice.
This pen is a special pen, it is the best in the land,
Every day this pen shines bright in your hand.
Never write without this pen,
For this is the special pen!

James Sadler (13)
Windsor High School, Halesowen

THE WRITE STUFF

Writing, writing black and blue
Writing, writing how'd you do?
Inks of all colours
Pens everywhere
Can you cope and not lose your hair?

Writing, writing, how do you cope?
Writing, writing, don't lose hope
Poems, stories all around
In the library don't make a sound
Books of 500 pages and more

How many books can you remember
Join a library, are you a member?
There are books around for all ages
Hurry up and turn those pages
I hope this poem has inspired you
Now go and write a poem too!

David Jackson (12)
Windsor High School, Halesowen

WRITING WRONGS

I'm right, you're wrong
I'm big, you're small
Mess with me
And you will see.

I'm right, you're wrong
You're weak, I'm strong
So shut your mouth
And bite your tongue!

We know I'm right
We know you're wrong
And there's nothing you
Can do about that
And that's a fact
So beat that.

Emily Goodman (13)
Windsor High School, Halesowen

MY SISTER

Where is my school pencil case?
I need it for today
It contains all my pens and pencils
Without it I'll be stuck.

My sister laughs and moves away
Whispering no such luck.

She's got my ruler in one hand
My sharpener in the other
I tell her to give them back
Or I'll go and tell our mother.

I try to gather my papers, books and my ink pen
Oh my rubber's lying on the floor
And then I start to count to ten.

My sister's realising I'm getting mad
She slowly hands my things back to me
At last I'm off to school now
But I'm dreading seeing my sister now at half-past three.

Samantha Dowler (13)
Windsor High School, Halesowen

THE WRITE STUFF

When I pick up my pen out of my pencil case
I feel like writing!
An urge streaks up my arm and I feel like writing!
Ideas are flooding into my head, gushing like a river
I put my pen on paper and start jotting!
The pen weaves across the paper like someone knitting blue colours
Ideas flow and lines and lines are being written
My pen is used for most things
My pen is very important
Because it's there at the most crucial moments when I need it
Sitting in my top pocket very cosy
It can be used for drawing and writing
After the gushing spree of writing I feel calm
And put my pen away.

Gavin Allsop (13)
Windsor High School, Halesowen

THE PENCIL

1

The pencil lies there motionless and still,
Thinking, I hope I'll be used, I hope I will,
The rubber's been rubbed at,
The pen's been used,
But there lies the poor pencil still unused.
The pencil lies still on that very same spot,
Getting cold in the winter and in the summer too hot.
Will anyone use that pencil again
Or will it lie there still, day after day?

Rachel Tuckey (12)
Windsor High School, Halesowen

216

SPORT, SPORT

Football, football
is really cool,
Tennis, tennis
is a menace,
Bowling, bowling
please stop moaning,
Darts, darts
will break your hearts.

Basketball, basketball
is played in the hall,
Hockey, hockey
I am a jockey,
Baseball, baseball
you are cruel,
There's my poem on sports,
I'm catching the ship to the ports.

Greg Parkes (13)
Windsor High School, Halesowen

FOOD

I'm writing about my food
It has a good taste
I love my food, it won't go to waste
I adore my food when it's on a big plate
There is not a food that I really hate
My food is cooked by my mother
I eat far more than my brother.
I like my food
It has a good *taste!*

Luke Hodgkins (12)
Windsor High School, Halesowen

PENCIL CASE

'Miss, my pencil case if full to the brim,
The colours inside are no way dim.
I've got pink, yellow, blue and black,
There isn't a colour, which I lack.
I've got glittery pencils and shiny pens
And a ruler covered with pictures of hens.
My rubber and sharpener are silver and gold
And my black marker writes really bold.
I've got Sellotape, scissors and Tipp-Ex too
And to stick stuff together, a tube of glue.
My little notebook is full of pictures
And all of me and my friend's fixtures.
Sam, my best, best mate,
Says my pencil case is great.
There is just one little problem with this,
My pencil case is at home, Miss.'

Abby Jones (12)
Windsor High School, Halesowen

LEARN TO WRITE

We learn to write when we are young
And not much sense it makes
To us it is a work of art
And a lot of hard work it takes.

We have to practise all day long
To get this looking right
First at school and then at home
Even if it takes all night.

And then those days have arrived
For exams we have to take
So we look back over the years
And I'm glad we learnt to write.

Alex Male (12)
Windsor High School, Halesowen

THE TEST

Pencil case out,
Pens out,
Pencils out,
Paper on the table,
What to write, I think?
It comes to me,
Start writing,
Halfway down the page,
Writer's cramp sets in,
Can't write any more,
Got to finish work,
Got to try,
Palms ache and wrists hurt,
Nearly finished now,
Got to finish, got to finish,
Need to finish, got to finish,
Finally . . . finished!
The pain stops,
Pens put away,
Pencils put away,
Work handed in!

Jon Rudge (12)
Windsor High School, Halesowen

MY HAND HURTS

My pen flows over my page, as my stories flow freely out of my brain.
My pencil flows over my page as pictures come onto the page to amaze.
There's just one thing you need to do, colour with gel pens, smelly
ones too.
Christmas, birthday, get well soon, all need a card sent to you.
On your hols in the sun, send a postcard to everyone, to tell them you're
having fun.

In the labs at school,
Bangs and smells,
Experiments,
We do answers and questions,
Conclusions we write to make everything alright.
Writing and writing all day long,
My pen's now run out,
The smelly ones too.
There's no lead in my pencils,
What shall I do?
Pack up and leave,
That's what I'll do.

Lucia Kleanthous (12)
Windsor High School, Halesowen

FRIENDS

You can feel happy, sad or angry,
But only a real friend would still be there for you.
You can rely on your friend with all your heart,
But only a real friend would be true.

You tell a friend your secrets,
They never hide the truth.
They help you through desperate times,
They are never miserable or uncouth.

A friend cares for you when you're upset,
A friend joins in when you're having fun.
Just make sure your friends are around you,
Remember, two heads are better than one.

Terri Akufo-Tetteh (14)
Windsor High School, Halesowen

THE WRITE BLEND

Write about poverty
Write about disease
Write about donkeys
Or write about sleaze

Novels about society
Novels about world peace
Novels about crustaceans
And one about a magic fleece

Poems about love
Poems about joy
Poems about sheep
And poems that don't rhyme

Songs that make you happy
Songs that make you cry
Songs that make no sense at all
Songs to say goodbye

Poems, novels, songs
Serious or not
Mix them together
What have you got?

This poem, that's what!

James Guggenheim (15)
Windsor High School, Halesowen

WRITE STUFF!

First lesson of the day - English
One of my favourite subjects
I hope I'm writing a story today
I have all my stationery and books waiting.

That lesson flew by! Now - maths
Calculator = percentages + decimals
Protractor x compass = angles
Ruler _____ straight lines = 180°

Guten Tag! (Hello, for you non-speaking Germans!)
Welcome to German. Pencils and pens are needed.
Have all my German vocabulary sheets and dictionaries out.
Ready to start the test . . .

The last lesson was history.
A colourful subject (felt tips and gel pens are required),
Packed away and waiting to go home.
All my things are ready to start a new day . . .

Megan David (12)
Windsor High School, Halesowen

MY FAVOURITE SAYINGS

Mom! Can I use the phone?
I promise I won't moan
Can I Mom, please?
I say all of these.

Mom, tell Rachel
I hate being small
Can I have some new clothes
I say all of those.

Rachel hurry up
Oi! That's my cup
That's my cheese
I say all of these.

Come on just pretend
Have you got a quid to lend
That's the one I chose
I say all of those.

Stephen Parsons (11)
Windsor High School, Halesowen

WRITE OR WRONG?

Write me a poem
My name's George
I'll phone the police
The poem is forged.

Give me a break
I'm not that man
The poem is fake
'C'mon son, get in the van.'

Prison is cruel
Why can't it be cool?
I committed the crime
Forced to do the time.

I wish I could talk
Just on the phone
Well, it's not just my fault
I didn't write the poem alone.

Michael Kendrick (15)
Windsor High School, Halesowen

THE WRITE STUFF

Pick up some paper,
Pick up a pen,
Think, think, tick-tock goes the clock, as you think, think,
Thought,
Touch the pen on the paper and move,
Making all squiggles and marks on the paper,
With the pen,
Like a painting, but in words.

The pen,
It moves all over the paper,
A mark here, a mark there,
Until they all make sense,
Like a painting, but in words.

The paper,
With blue and black all over it covering that snow-white colour,
The swirls and curls
And the straight, sharp lines,
Keep going, keep going,
Until they all have a significant meaning,
Like a painting, but in words.

Daniel Bath (12)
Windsor High School, Halesowen

QUALITIES OF ENGLISH

The tip slightly touched the paper
Like two people holding hands.
The slight drop of ink ruins the plain snow-white paper
Like dark black oil in a light blue ocean.

Each letter one by one
Like people queuing up, all with different features.
Maybe an excellent cover but what's inside?
Don't judge a book by its cover!

Edward Freeth (11)
Windsor High School, Halesowen

THE WRITE STUFF

Paper, pens and pencils,
that's what I use to write,
to write an interesting story,
by day or by night.
I look down at my blank paper
and considered to write a date,
then I write my title
and give it to my mate.
Then I slowly begin to write my story,
always looking back,
then I take a red pen
out of my backpack.

Then I cross out my mistake
and change it so it's right,
then I carry on my story
writing into the night.
When I finish writing my story,
then I'll hand it in,
then I'll take my wrong work
and I'll put it in the bin.

Gemma Basterfield (12)
Windsor High School, Halesowen

My Mom!

She's nice, she's lovely, she's the best.
She's like a bird nesting her little ones
Then going out to get the food.
She spreads the butter on my bread,
She mashes my potatoes,
She boils my egg,
She looks after me day and night, night and day.
When she walks into a room I always say, 'I love you.'
She's that special one
My mom!

Jodie Leonard-Gair (12)
Windsor High School, Halesowen

Write, Write, Write

Write, write, write is all I ever do
And when you don't the teacher looks at you
Write, write, write is all I ever learn
No time to stop and turn
Write, write, write is all I do all day
No time to stop and play
Write, write, write my friends do it too
How about you?
Write, write, write, stop!

Daniel Hamblett (12)
Windsor High School, Halesowen

The Write Stuff

Rubbers, sharpeners and coloured pencils,
Coloured pens and drawing stencils.
All of these things we use every day,
To make our work look neat in every way.

Protractors and scissors to cut and measure,
Coloured gel pens we use for pleasure.
We write to our friends with all our news,
But 'cause stationery's small, it's easy to lose!

Melissa Richardson (12)
Windsor High School, Halesowen

CRIME AND RIGHTS

They riot through the streets at night,
The glass of a shop window is obliterated
And the shop alarm yells,
The robbers steal stuff from the shop,
They run, run down a dark alley,
Dark and gloomy . . .
They see a red light,
Boom!
Pinned against the wall,
A voice, it says, 'You have the *right* to remain silent!'

Thomas Attwood (12)
Windsor High School, Halesowen

THE RIGHT STUFF

Murdering someone, right or wrong?
Fighting for your country, right or wrong?
Stealing for someone, right or wrong?
Helping someone, right or wrong?

Tom Pearson (12)
Windsor High School, Halesowen

THE OUTCAST

At last! I'm bought with my friends,
I hope using my ink never ends,
My smooth casing shall never break
And my spring will never stop bouncing.

Oh, my owner's opening my bed I lie in,
She's taking my friend just to write with,
OK, it's me next,
Actually, it's my other friend.

I'm the last in the package,
I'm definitely next,
I'll be put in her amazing case,
With rainbow pens, just like me.

Why is she walking off without me?
She's turning off the light,
She's locking the door with a key,
Why am I all alone?

Sylvia Quek (12)
Windsor High School, Halesowen

WRITING ABOUT WRONGS

Bodies flung everywhere,
As if with no care.
Right or wrong?
From the war on Iraq,
To getting the sack.
Right or wrong?

Killing for fun.
Killing with guns.
Right or wrong?
Bodies hung everywhere,
As if with no care,
Right or wrong?

James Washbrook (12)
Windsor High School, Halesowen

THE WRITE STUFF

The pages are blank,
The lines are blue,
I need to write a story,
But I don't know what to do!

My pen is clicking,
The clock is too,
I need to write an essay,
But I don't know what to do!

My brain's not working,
How will I get through?
I need to write a poem,
But I don't know what to do!

The pages are blank,
The lines are blue,
I need to write a story
But I don't know what to do!

Richard Seeley (12)
Windsor High School, Halesowen

THE WRITE STUFF

Have you got the write stuff?
Have you got the cool stuff?

The write stuff's a PlayStation
The write stuff's a phone
The write stuff's a Game Boy
And ho, ho, ho!

The write stuff's a holiday
The write stuff's music
The write stuff's trainers
And a bottle of rum

The write stuff's a roster
The write stuff's a yo-yo
The write stuff's a fork
And a pile of loot.

James Workman (11)
Windsor High School, Halesowen

MY MIND IS BLANK!

We've been told a poem,
We have to write.
So I think and I think,
With all my might.

All I need,
Are some words that rhyme.
Throw them together
And it should be just fine!

Philip Long (13)
Windsor High School, Halesowen

FOR KATIE ELIZABETH

The black branches of Winter's grip clamber and grab into
the pallid skies,
Tiny sprinkles of frost litter the grass, glinting in the sun that
the wispy clouds try to hide.

Then the darkness and blue freeze is gone and the rebirth
of refreshing spring takes hold,
Blasts of bright yellow, fresh green and sparkling dew
and the birth of all sorts of babies too.

Now my friends, after your first tiny angels of autumn,
comes Katie Elizabeth, born like the tenderness of spring,
But her precious years will soon fly by for they grow so fast
at this wonderful time of life.
Keep the nostalgia and true good times close and try not to break
the family's never-ending circle of love and hope.

So for now dear friends all you need ponder is the tiny details in life
only a parent and their child can see,
Such as pirates or monsters even that rhyme of the three shopkeepers
lost at sea.

As you lay her down to bed, sit for a while as she sleeps
and think to yourself, *what's going on in your head?*
Take every tiny detail down in your mind even when she's naughty
and you see red, or as she weeps and cries.

Then lay back and remember to yourself in the times of cold
to never break that single tender hold.

Sarah Kelly Bemand (15)
Windsor High School, Halesowen

THE WRITE STUFF

The write stuff is mobiles,
The write stuff is McDonald's,
The write stuff is jeans
And don't forget trainers.

The write things are denims,
The write things are CDs,
The write things are good bags
And don't forget hairstyles.

The write holiday equipment,
The write pencil case,
The write clothes
And don't forget the write friends.

Amy Savin (11)
Windsor High School, Halesowen

THAT GIRL IN MY ROAD

There's a girl in my road you know
She's got all the right stuff
She can't help getting all the good stuff.

She's got all the right stuff for school
And at home she has a really good pool
She has all the right stuff which is so cool.

She lives in a big house
As a pet she has a really small mouse
She's the coolest girl I know
The only thing is I don't know her name!

Charlotte Harris (11)
Windsor High School, Halesowen

THE WRITE STUFF

T he write stuff is really
H ard but it's really
E asy for me because I know

W hat to do, but the thing is it is always
R ight, the teachers give me merits, they say I am really
I mportant because I don't ever
T alk but everybody
E lse is talking through the lesson, they say I'm

S pectacular
T o do everything they want me to do
U ntil the day we break up the
F unny thing is it's
F antastic because I can be as naughty as I want.

Jodie Pawlowski (11)
Windsor High School, Halesowen

THE WRITE STUFF

There's a boy in our class with all the write stuff
Pens, pencils and rulers, he can't get enough
He's good at every sport, he goes to a club
And for all his medals he's got a big tub
He wears the write stuff with the right rips and tears
Even his mum wears her old pair of flares
He's got a CD Walkman with loads of CDs
He's really smart and sharp and has never had fleas
His watches are digital, his hair is cut short
And in his exams, he's never got nought
There's a boy in our class with all the write stuff
Pens, pencils and rulers, he can't get enough.

Magnus Silverwood (11)
Windsor High School, Halesowen

THE WRITE STUFF

T   ell me to write once more and I'll scream

H ow much more can I take?

E   very day it's write this, write that, write the other.

W ell I'm telling you, I'm not going to stand it

R emember, I've got the power to get you sacked

I   'll do it, I will, I really will

T   ime's running out you say and I say not

E   ach time I threaten you, you say, 'So what!'

S   o I'll have to try harder I suppose

T   ut, it's not fair

U nfair, I say, unfair, unfair, unfair

F   ace it, I'll get even, I will

F   ace it, I'll get even, I will, I will, I will.

Jessica Billage (11)
Windsor High School, Halesowen

THE RIGHT CLASSROOM

The whiteboard sits all alone
As kids get out their phones.
Teachers tell us what to do
When we graffiti something new.
Ink pens fly through the air
As we come up with a new dare.
Then we get out our books ready to write
When we talk about the next fight
Everything in this classroom is very right
It's best when everyone's gone at night.

Jackson Rees (12)
Windsor High School, Halesowen

WRITING OF HOW NOTHING GOES RIGHT

Nothing goes right
Everything goes wrong
This dark age of gloom
Seems so long

I feel like I'm in the dark
Pushed out of the light
Nothing in my life
Seems to go right

Hurtful words
Every day
I sometimes wish
I could fly away

Crying all day
Crying all night
I wish something
For once would go right.

Liza Bicknell (12)
Windsor High School, Halesowen

MR RIGHT

My Mr Right would be a writer
Dark hair, dark eyes, skin tone lighter
Tall, strong, writing a song
Kind, nice and caring
Singing all day long.

Kirsty Louise Patchett (12)
Windsor High School, Halesowen

THE RIGHT STUFF GANG

You've got to have the right stuff in my gang,
Or you will be out in a bang,
If your trainers aren't Adidas or Nike,
If you don't have a BMX bike.

If you don't stay at home alone
And you do not have a Nokia phone,
If you don't wear chains or earrings
And you do not have all the right things.

If you don't listen to So Solid Crew
And you do not know what to do,
If you don't have a good hairstyle
And you haven't visited the River Nile.

Then you haven't got what it takes to be in my gang.

Daniel Hadley (11)
Windsor High School, Halesowen

THE WRITE AND WRONG STUFF

Is it right to kill someone
Or is it wrong?
Is it wrong to go to war
Or is it right?
Mr Blair thinks so.

Is it right to go to school
Or is it wrong?
Should I skive
Or should I try and belong?

Mark Chatterley (12)
Windsor High School, Halesowen

THE RIGHT STUFF!

Wow, I need the latest hairstyle
Yes, I need the right clothes
Cool, that's a wicked mobile phone
Fantastic, I like this new CD
Quick, I need the right look
Mom, this is all the right uniform
Now, look at these new football boots
Safe, I love that brand new mountain bike
Yes, I'm getting all this make-up
Please, it means a lot to me
Thank you, these trainers are divine
Nice, look at my behaviour isn't it really good?
Mom and Dad, get me the right stuff.

Hannah Alboreky (11)
Windsor High School, Halesowen

WRITING ABOUT PANTS IS *PANTS!*

The right pants are pants for me
I make sure they're not small and itchy
As I write I ponder pants
What are the right pants for me?

If I were a girl I'd wear a tight thong
But would it hurt my *ding dong?*
Please, please, please
Find the right pants for me
So I can be at ease
As I write cool poetry!

Josh Brinksman (12)
Windsor High School, Halesowen

WHICH WAY IS RIGHT, WHICH WAY IS WRONG?

As I write this poem I ponder . . .
Which way's right, which way's wrong?
Around every corner that I turn there's a story that needs to unfold
In every direction that I look
There's people to see and places to go
There's a path to take, which one? Which one's right,
Which one's wrong?
Around every corner, there's right and there's wrong,
Sometimes you take the wrong path and make a mistake,
A mistake is waiting for everyone
So take the path, the road, you think is best
And remember not to look behind but to look to the future
Just say this question in your head, which way's right,
Which way's wrong?

Victoria Potter (12)
Windsor High School, Halesowen

THE WRITE STUFF!

The write stuff we use it every day
without it there would be no letters,
words, poems and stories.
Authors of the world need the right stuff
to create masterpieces.
With the right stuff imagination can run wild
and become a gateway to the perfect world.
We write and write to our heart's
content but some day they shall work no more!

Tom Tromans & Tom Fathers (12)
Windsor High School, Halesowen

WRITE STUFF

W ith all the equipment needed you need the write stuff,
R eally when you haven't got the write stuff you shouldn't
    get in a huff.
I n English, maths, geography and other subjects too,
T he write stuff is what you need to do what you have to do.
E very school, every day, there's always some,

S illy person with a lame excuse as to why it did not come.
T omorrow just because you haven't brought it doesn't mean
    you should have a fit.
U nder all the pressure just bring it.
F unny people just want to bluff,
F or your own sake remember to bring, the write stuff!

Andrew Preddy (12)
Windsor High School, Halesowen

WRITING

Flowing letters
Followed by a full stop.
A capital letter starts a new line.

Flowing letters
Small and large
Round and fat.

Flowing letters
All in a row
This is writing

And that's how it goes.

Eric Rowley (12)
Windsor High School, Halesowen

THE WRITE STUFF!

By putting pen upon the paper
With sturdy finger, words will taper.

Sloping or upright, capitals or small
The writing with pen on paper clearly describes it all.

Left hand, right hand whichever hand we use
The writing on the paper will be whatever words we choose.

Long words or short words,
Sentence or rhyme, the use of pen on paper,
Is proved on every line.

There are pencils and fountain pens, biro with a ball
With either in hand moved across paper
The writing is proven to all.

Stephanie Churms (12)
Windsor High School, Halesowen

FROM STONES TO PENS

Writing began with picture-writing on cave walls,
Real writing began with the Romans and Egyptians
Who kept records.
In the future we wrote with pens on paper,
The most famous pens were the quills from feathers of birds,
Even today writing is developing,
As new countries form.
So do languages
And some languages die,
Like Latin.

Scott Coleman (12)
Windsor High School, Halesowen

MY DAY

After you kick-flip a 3 set,
You nollie on a trolley,
But everything else you ollie,
You hard-flip a 3 set,
For a bet,
You heel-flip a pod,
Just like a rod,
My mate's being hip,
While I casper-flip,
You get caught by the cops,
Doing the drops,
There's nowhere to SK8!
But it's getting late,
It's about 8,
So as you head home,
After you kick-flip a 3 set
That's my day!

Niall Patterson (13)
Windsor High School, Halesowen

WRITING ABOUT MR RIGHT

Dark hair, dark eyes
That is how I imagine Mr Right
Tall, strong and extremely buff
Kind, nice but a little bit tough
That's the man that's right for me
Mr Right, as perfect as can be.

Charlotte Thompson (12)
Windsor High School, Halesowen

Mr And Mrs Right Are Writing

We are Mr and Mrs Right
We never ever fight
We get on very, very well
We keep our secrets
And never ever tell.

Mr and Mrs Right
We never ever fight
We have two children
Called Richard and Mildred
Who we love with all our heart
We will never ever part.

Mr and Mrs Right
We never ever fight
We are always together
Whatever the outdoor weather.

Rachel Deakin & Carla Moskot-Brettell (12)
Windsor High School, Halesowen

The Write Stuff

Is it right when people are bad, they should go to jail?
Is it right that I should be able to learn things at school and others can't?
Is it right that some people hurt innocent animals?
Is it right that some people have houses and other people don't?
Is it right that some people with similar jobs get paid more?
Is it right that some are more equal than others?

Harrison Bishop (13)
Windsor High School, Halesowen

SHIP MAKER

I wish I was a ship maker
And helped to build big ships
I would meet up with all my mates
And we would go on trips.

These ships are really heavy
We build them really tough
So they are not damaged in rough seas
We make them from the right stuff.

Passengers sail on these ships
They travel near and far
Some people fly by aeroplane
Others go by car.

Thomas Flavell (12)
Windsor High School, Halesowen

THE WRITE STUFF

Heart beats swiftly,
Pens write steadily,
Silence in the classroom,
Students working their hardest,
Blank faces
Amongst understanding ones.

Tables shaking
As pens start aching,
Tension in the classroom
As paragraphs get completed,
Stories begin, stories end,
Everyone puts down their pens.

Katy Piller (11)
Windsor High School, Halesowen

WHAT'S THE RIGHT THINGS?

I'm by the door
Ring the bell, he opens the door
I call him a boar
I run away
He yells, 'You'll pay!'
I'm not sure
Whether I'll knock that door
I know I was wrong
No, I won't knock that door
Two wrongs don't make a right.

I go to that door
I want to say sorry
I knock on that door
No answer
I walk away
I never got to say
Sorry!

Daniel Williams (12)
Windsor High School, Halesowen

THE WRITE STUFF!

Is it right to go to school
Or is it wrong?
No!
Is it wrong to read and write,
Or is it right?
Yes!
Is it right to make your own choice
Or is it wrong to take others' advice?
Maybe!

Daniel Cash (13)
Windsor High School, Halesowen

AS I WRITE

I open my book to a clean, white page,
The view is as white as the winter's snow.
My pen touches the snowy scene,
The ink flows out.
The words start to appear,
Letter by letter like black little men linking up together.
The ink wrecks the winter view,
It looks like slush on the snowy page.

My hand swiftly moves across the page.
I stop writing for a while,
I think really hard what to write
An idea pops into my head.
I write it down before it runs out of my brain.
At last I'm on my last line.
My pen stops working.
I've finished.
I put my pen away.
That's a lesson gone, just two more to go.

Natalie Young (13)
Windsor High School, Halesowen

THE WRITE STUFF

Racing in my immaculate, red sports car
90mph or more,
Going through red lights,
I don't care even if I am breaking the law,
I've gone out of control,
Twisting and turning,
Swerving and curving,
Boom!

Matthew Hipkiss (13)
Windsor High School, Halesowen

My Family

When I write about my family I think of
The good times.
But sometimes the bad
My mom, my dad and my horrible, older brother,
The family I live with whether I like it or not.
I have a good time when I'm out and about,
But only with them.
A bad time is when they're not with me
And I'm alone.
We can always do something right.
I hate it when it's wrong.
I love my family,
I think they're great,
Because they're always there for me.

James Reece (12)
Windsor High School, Halesowen

Neat Copy

W hen the teams make their way out of the changing rooms
R *ush, rush, rush* goes the cleaner's broom.
I nformation where the teams will stand,
T ime before they hear the marching band.
E lectrifying noise from the enormous crowd!

S econds later came out the teams,
T he light manufacturer puts on the beams
U nfortunately the game is unfinished
F ortunately there's no one banished . . .
F inished.

Ben Ebanks (12)
Windsor High School, Halesowen

THE STATIONERY SHOP

I go to the stationery shop
And there I stop
To look at pencils and pens
And there I spend
A lot of money
On pens smelling of honey.

I also buy
An ink pen and rubber
And get told off by my mother
For spending all of my pocket money
On a pen that smells of honey.

Lucy Sidaway (12)
Windsor High School, Halesowen

THE ENGLISH ROSE OF RUGBY

I do like other sports - but rugby is my game
Football is OK, but I'll take rugby just the same
I love the tackling and the scrums - yes, rugby is my game
Even though at times it hurts, but hey, no pain, no gain!
I wish I could play all the time - rugby is my game
Because I don't mind playing in the sun, the wind or rain
I would love to play at Twickenham - oh rugby is my game
Yes, running out in an England shirt - that is my aim
And when I score that winning try - in rugby that's my game
Someone would ask my dad, 'Who's that?'
And he would say, 'Joe Townsend is his name!'

Joe Townsend (13)
Windsor High School, Halesowen

WRITING TOGETHER

When I write, you write too
Right, let's start, me and you
I'll start to write then you can too
We'll gain more strength
Working as a crew
Writing words
Creating songs
Sharing feelings
When I write, you write too,
Read and write
Right and wrong
Which one is the right one?
Think
Think along with me,
Together we will always be
Strong.

Sophie James (12)
Windsor High School, Halesowen

THE WRITE STUFF

There's a girl
in our class
that's got all
the best stuff.
She's got trainers
and medals and
a pencil case
full of the
write stuff.

Sara Priest (11)
Windsor High School, Halesowen

THE WRITE STUFF

Stationery is a useful tool,
Used every day in and out of school.
Writing, colouring, drawing too,
Pens, pencils, rubbers for me and you.

Rulers used for underlining,
Making work neat and tidy.
Protractors, calculators used in maths for adding and measuring angles.

Stationery everywhere, used every day,
We couldn't do without it.
All kinds of stationery, so many to think of.
So many to use in different ways,
So many to use every day.

Katie Pearson (12)
Windsor High School, Halesowen

LIKE THIS, LIKE THAT, AS GOOD AS THIS

As right as rain
As wrong as no
As up as sky
As fast as go.

As tough as nails
As soft as soup
As short as shoes
As long as rope.

As nice as pie
As good as gold
As smooth as new
As rough as old.

Kelly Bradbrook (12)
Windsor High School, Halesowen

THE WRITE STUFF

Do you have the right school equipment?
Pens, pencils, felts and a rubber too!
What about your pencil case?
Is it big, is it small, is it just the right size for you?
Is it what you like?

How about your uniform?
Do you look smart, is your shirt tucked in?
Is your tie the right length?
Have you got suitable shoes,
No slippery snakes, I hope!

If you've got the write stuff,
I'm sure you'll cope just fine!

Kaylee Mallin (12)
Windsor High School, Halesowen

AS I WRITE, WRONG IS RIGHT

When you are faced with wrong or right,
Try to keep this in your sight,
When you are faced with right or wrong,
The black ink night it seems so long,
I then remember somebody said,
That all is wrong is in your head,
And all the time that you be led.
It could mean that you feel dead (inside),
Take heart my friend
And take my ear that you can bend
And know that with me right or wrong
You will always have a loving friend.

Che Miller (12)
Windsor High School, Halesowen

WRITING ABOUT MY LISP

I have a lisp,
I sound like a hissing snake,
I can't say an S,
Or sometimes an R,
When I say something wrong,
It might just be right,
Because with my lisp you never know,
You could say something you never wanted to,
But sometimes you know, I don't mind
Either my words are right or wrong,
But I do know that you will know,
About my lisp and so, so, so,
Although you can hear it when I talk,
You cannot hear it when I write.

Sam Cole (12)
Windsor High School, Halesowen

JUMBLED UP WRITING

We write, write, write
Till our hand is sore
We write, write, write
Till the page is torn
We write, write, write
Till our head explodes
We write *italic*
We write *bold*
We write all day
We write all night
And then again tomorrow night
We write, write, write.

Lucy Rudge (12)
Windsor High School, Halesowen

YE OLDE ENGLISH

Shakespeare, now there's a clever man,
His play scripts, they never thought to ban
And Dickens, writing 'A Christmas Carol',
They both wrote stories by the barrel.
With tales that cause your imagination to spark,
Under the covers, with a torch in the dark.

Just float away in-between the words
And transport yourself to other worlds,
One moment you could solve a crime,
The next you might be covered in slime,
For all these books are make-believe,
You never know what's up their sleeve.

They make you cry, and make you scared
And best of all, they can be shared,
They all have an interesting plot,
Just so that, they don't get forgot,
If you haven't realised, take a look,
I'll think you'll find, I'm talking about books!

Books can help you comprehend,
What may be sending a friend round the bend,
Bullying, teasing, taunting and hate,
All of these can be expressed to your mate,
Books can show you the damage they can do,
So help your friend, it's up to you.

In books the end, is usually happy,
But your friend may not end up being a smiling chappie.
So help him out and in the end
You will end up being a better friend,
For books have taught us many great things
And we all deserve, to feel like kings.

Nick Slater (13)
Windsor High School, Halesowen

POEMS

R idiculous as Richard is,
I think I might just be able to write a poem about it.
C omplex this puzzle really is,
H ow am I to accomplish this?
A s I am useless at writing poems any way,
R hyming is almost impossible but at least I know when I'm
D efeated.

N ot another blasted poem!
I 've had enough of these,
C odswallop is my opinion of my poems,
H aven't you realised that yet?
O ther people's poems are far better,
L ook at those, not this.
L ife's too short to look at my poems,
S pend it some other way.

Richard Nicholls (13)
Wrekin College, Telford

SMILE

Smile happily
Happily laugh
Laugh loud
Loud mouth
Mouths eat
Eat food
Food tasty
Tasty sweets
Sweet smile
Smile happily.

Emma Price (13)
Wrekin College, Telford

WATER

The cold, damp water, so crystal clear,
It flows around so calmly,
It's quiet, it's gentle,
It hardly makes a sound,
As the sunlight shines upon the water's face,
The water glitters and gleams,
When you drink the water on a hot summer's day.
It quenches your thirst so quickly.
But this water can become fierce
When it crashes against the sharp, jagged rocks
And water engulfing anything in sight.
It roars and smashes
As the waves start to come
And lightning crashes.
Now the rapids start to appear,
The water is not always the place to be.
It's now quiet
And waves have gone.
The sky is no longer grey
And now it's quiet, so very quiet.
It feels that the waves never came
And now the sun comes out
And now it is no longer as fierce as it once became.

Jonathan Price (13)
Wrekin College, Telford

THE RAGING RIVER

How calm it was, how fierce it is.
How slow and gentle it was, how fast and raging it is.
How danger-free then, how *dangerous* now.
Oh how different it seems to how it used to be.
How it used to give life and now how it steals it.

How it was the source of life and now it feeds on it.
It used to attract so many people but now it does the opposite
But still people come to be engulfed by its mighty power.
We tell them to go but faith calls them ever closer,
Closer to the life-eating creature that is our river.

Alex Llewellyn (13)
Wrekin College, Telford

WAITING

The monstrous water raging along,
Swallowing everything in its path.
Roaring like a monster beneath the river bed,
Waiting for a tasty human to land in his trap.
As the monster sees his prey,
Swimming along his gentle belly.
It grabs his prey and takes him hurtling
Down the river, drowning his prey.
Engulfing anything in his path.
As his prey slowly loses his breath,
Gasping for more and more air,
Slowly, slowly running out.
Then the prey dies.
The beast sucks his breath dry.
Then the beast returns,
Pretending nothing happened.
Turning into a calm river,
Slowly slowing down.
River enjoying its surroundings
Until another prey lands into
His evil trap.
Waiting, waiting.

Luke Matthews (13)
Wrekin College, Telford

THE FEELINGS OF A TEENAGE GIRL

I   like him

T   hough I don't think he likes me
H   e likes *her*
I   like him so much
N   othing could change the way I feel
K   nowing he likes me would make my life complete

I   like him so much

A   ll I ever think about is him
M   aybe he does like me, there is always hope

I   like him more than anything
N   othing could tear me away from him

L   iking someone is an amazing feeling, but
O   nly when the love is reciprocated
V   ery strong is my love for him
E   very day it grows stronger.

Nicola Jones (14)
Wrekin College, Telford

THE INNOCENCE OF A HUMBLE FLOWER

The innocence of a humble flower,
The sweet smelling air,
Its petals open into the breeze,
With nobility at its brow.

The innocence of a humble flower,
It surely must be seen,
It shoots up into the great blue yonder
And becomes an entire bloom.

The innocence of a humble flower,
Amongst the long green grass.
It greets the nearby deep blue sea
With a cheery hello bounce.

The innocence of a humble flower,
It stands up tall and straight,
Battling the wind, it falls,
No more a beautiful flower, its dignity shattered.

Ben Tufft
Wrekin College, Telford

A DIFFERENT VIEW

What do I begin with?
Where do I start?
How do I spell?
It may be easy for you
But not for me.
You take it for granted.
An endless struggle
Remembering how to spell.
I can't see the patterns
Or hear the sounds like you.
It slows you down
And trips you up.
Always rushing;
Never first in the written race.
Others are finished
When I am still wondering.
Perhaps one day you will understand
How difficult it was for me to write.

Clare Harnell (12)
Wrekin College, Telford

THE FUTURE

How will it be in the future?
Will people still go to school?
If we did, would there be robots
To stop people playing the fool?

Would we still drive cars,
An aeroplane, train or bus?
What if we started to teleport,
Wouldn't it be a fuss?

What will become of books,
TV, music or fame?
Will we still have banks with money?
Will it change or be the same?

What will become of the starving?
What will happen to the ill?
Will there be a cure for cancer
In something as small as a pill?

So will the world have changed for the better
Or will it just be a mess?
Will it be a wondrous place?
We'll just have to wonder and guess!

Jenny Alman (13)
Wrekin College, Telford

THE CHEETAH

He lies there in the grass,
    invisible to the last,
Soon will come the day,
    when he seeks his prey.

Eventually comes the day,
   when he sees his prey,
He will no longer stay,
   but chase and kill his prey.

James Jemmett (14)
Wrekin College, Telford

OUR CURSE OF DEATH

Her scream was shrill,
Outside there was a chill.
The lightning struck,
She ran out of luck.

Displayed on the mud,
Was her ruby-red blood.
There she was buried,
Away the crooks scurried.

Fourteen long years,
Did it take for her family and peers,
To find her body rotten,
Wrapped in white cotton.

All they found were her bones,
There they heard the sound of moans.
The clouds turned a stormy black,
Her frightened screams came back.

A plague of disease descended upon the town,
Everyone and everything began to drown.
The people began to cry,
'Was this the way we were to die?'

Sonja Randhawa (13)
Wrekin College, Telford

Rain

As I fall and fall
Faster, falling, tumbling into this harsh world
Faster and faster.
Then it happens, the raindrops dread it
Cold, so cold.
I had turned into a snowflake.
Some say I look mysterious, others, strange.
I think strange.
As we land on the fresh grass
Ready to be squashed by more unfortunate snow.
The sun,
Oh the sun, scorching, burning sun.
Melting, changing, evaporating,
Dying,
Being eaten, swallowed by this harsh world.
But then I was safe in the moving clouds.
My house, my home.
Only to be resting, waiting till the cloud goes black
And then it would happen again, it would *rain!*

James Pickering (13)
Wrekin College, Telford

Our Sea

Water, water, everywhere
78 percent of the world is water.
Creatures dwell in the sea.
Sea is like polish, it sweeps the world clean.
Waves are hands that clean the shores.
Smooth like magic.
Sea is a home to keep the world clean.

James Henderson (12)
Wrekin College, Telford

SWEETS

The glossed eye-blinding colours
Hang in the window -
Shining strawberry-reds,
Glistening apple-greens,
Crisp yellows,
Rich, superior purples,
Staring down at me,
Entrancing me,
I feel the sweet thrill,
Tingling on my tongue -
Mouth-watering sensations
Draw me to them.
I reach out -
Needing the splendour in my hand.
I rip them off the shelf,
What should I do?
Panicked, I rip off the top of the packet
And throw a sweet into my mouth.
Bitterness fills my sensations,
The thrill evaporates -
The colours fade.

Peter Bunn (13)
Wrekin College, Telford

WATER

Water, anywhere,
Water, frozen into ice
A bit like a water device.
Water can be as hot as a pan.
Does it sparkle like fire?

Laura Nichols (11)
Wrekin College, Telford

EMPTY WATER

Seeing the water
flowing by, then seeing
something but just a little fly
Swimming slowly above
the rocks and just seeing
someone and had a big shock.
Not seeing someone for a while
she walked up in a certain style.
She peered cautiously into the water
and then regretting, I should have caught her.
Walking away without a care and then
giving her a little stare.
Sitting there forever and ever, feeling like
I want to sever and then starting to be aware
of the weather, I searched
desperately for a fish and then
praying for a wish, but
nothing would come, which
is lucky for some.

Ashley Campbell (12)
Wrekin College, Telford

CRYSTALS SMASH

Crystals smash, water can,
Waterfalls fall falling, falling, falling
That's what they're made for
Water can talk if you walk it.

Water is cool
Water is tall
Water, it can be a wall.
Unless you treat it!

Finally we come to the end.
The estuary.
The water is to be left in peace.
So let it sleep.

Lewis Benson (11)
Wrekin College, Telford

My Friend The River

Every so often I have to escape,
Escape from everything.
I sit down next to the calm and gentle river
It seems to relate to me.
I can go and think,
Think freely.

The river doesn't comment on what I say,
Yet its stillness gives me faith.
Faith that it listens to me.
I never have to lie to the river
'Cause I know I can trust it.
Trust its calm, gentle, loving crystal-clear water.

The river would never judge me
And I would never make the river mad
Because that is not how I treat my friend.

I have come here since I was just a little girl.
This was my special place.

But people move on,
Friends move away
And yet I always know right where my friend will be.

Kathryn Zoulias (13)
Wrekin College, Telford

A BLOOD-RED MOON

As the darkness drew on, the battle began
At first it seemed never ending
But then a change - I could see blood-red
The colour of defeat was spreading.
Slowly, but surely the invaders were winning
As I peered out I was surprised -
A red rash floating across the sky.
The battle half-finished came to a stop,
Then started again and again and then not.
As the minutes drew on I knew who had won -
It was the invaders.
They left a stain of blood across space,
It still comes once in a while,
Next time I see it up in the sky,
Someone might ask, 'Who am I?'

Eve Barraclough (13)
Wrekin College, Telford

THE SWORDFISH

Swordfish, swordfish, we live in the salty sea
we're scaly, slimy, we sleep under the rocks.
Fishermen's nets we hate, other fish we eat.
Snaffling up the quicksilver fish,
then sleeping on the sandy sea floor.

Oil slick, oil slick, suddenly darkness, suddenly danger.
The slippery, sticky slick slides over us.

Charles Milner (12)
Wrekin College, Telford

THE PEBBLE

'I like that pebble,' I say.
'What pebble are you talking about?' she said.
'That pebble, my pebble.'
'There are many of them,' she said.
She then left.

Another one came.

'I like that pebble,' I say.
'What pebble are you talking about?' she said.
'That pcbble, my pebble.'
'There are many of them,' she said.
She then left.

I stared at the pebble in my hand.
'You still like it don't you?'
'They're all the same.'

Michael Reynolds
Wrekin College, Telford

FROSTBITE

Quietly it falls on a cold winter's night,
lying on the grass to the early morning light.
In the early morning it sparkles like glass,
as it lies silently on a blade of grass.
Next day it will be gone,
not a cloud in the sky, not a single one.
All the frost is departing . . . leaving . . .
as it travels down the drain.
It gurgles, always the same.

Alex Baker (12)
Wrekin College, Telford

ANGELS' FOUNTAINS

Water trickles through mountains,
Spurting out like fountains.
Water carves rocks and many years it takes to do this.
White ponies dancing on air,
Very beautiful to be fair.

When all together it's pandemonium,
Leaving a layer of dirt and scum.
Crashing into rocks of sheer size,
Though water spilled with oil, I do despise.
Mere human beings see water as a wet mess,
This is no ordinary test.

People think not of water and are not aware of their luckiness.
We must keep its cleanness and purity
For this water we have fought
And that's an encouraging thought.

David Higginbotham (13)
Wrekin College, Telford

SEA CREATURES

A huge killer whale
Chasing a catfish's tail.
Snapping his jaws
At the catfish's paws.

A speedy little fish
Thinking about his wish
To be free
In the deep blue sea.

A huge old tortoise
Overtaken by a porpoise
Swimming past
Leaving the tortoise last.

Edward Burn (12)
Wrekin College, Telford

THE WHEEL OF LIFE

The wheel of life is harsh,
For you don't know where it's going,
Stand in the wind,
For it is the voice of someone,
But who?

The wheel of life is harsh,
For it grabs you by the wrist,
Stand in the path of smoke,
For it is the scent of Hell,
But, is there a Hell, a God?

The wheel of life is harsh,
For it throws you into darkness,
Just look around,
People playing, flowers growing,
How can this world be real?

What would happen if we knew the answer?
Would the world change or race into badness?
So many questions are among us, can we answer any?
For are the answers deep somewhere, or are they just nearby?
Life is a question that will never be known, unless you just ask why?

The wheel of life is harsh,
But it is in your hands.

Harry Beirne (13)
Wrekin College, Telford

BUBBLING BLUE SEA

The bulging, bubbly, bashing, bold, blue sea
Swept against the pure shores of a sunny, sandy beach.

And then *crash, bang, wallop*, suddenly
The storm hits and in goes me!

The seagull sits on the stormy sea,
Where the waves go *swish, swish, wallop, swish.*

The sea is a bundle of water and waves,
Where people go swimming if they are brave.

The sea is a home for fishes and things.
Some boats mess around on the water top.

I'm sure the sea doesn't like it much,
I hope one day the sea gets its way.

And that's all I have to say!

Zara Bannister (11)
Wrekin College, Telford

THE KESTREL

All through the night
He roosts in dreamy slumber,
Waiting for the dawn to come,
His wings tucked under him,
Head down in sleep
Like a monk in prayer.
As the morning sun breaks, he lifts his head,

He takes to the air with wings stretching out
Like the flowers in the morning reaching for the sun.
He hovers high above the fields,
Eyes like glittering stars.
He spots a small movement in the grass,
He starts to descend
And without any sound
He strikes.

Oliver Todd (13)
Wrekin College, Telford

POEMS FROM THE BLUE PLANET

The powerful creature propels through the sea,
Tearing apart all in his way.
The creature is harmless to you and to me,
Yet a beast is too strong for those innocent fish.

In the crystal-clear blue sea,
Poachers hunt the beautiful underwater creature
But he is too quick for the weak and fearful mammals.

Now the creature is getting angry,
Those poachers moving in on his territory.
Running his domain so he then makes a move
And pulls on the fishing net with tormenting teeth.

His plan works with great trepidation,
One of the poachers falls in.
He quickly powers through the sea towards him
And then tears him apart - he dies in agony.

Katherine Gabb (11)
Wrekin College, Telford

THE MOTHER'S HORROR

A mother was bathing her baby one night
the youngest of ten, a tiny young mite
the mother was poor, the babe was thin
only a skeleton covered in skin.

The mother looked round, the baby had gone,
she cried and cried, she thought he had died.

She thought he had fallen down the plughole
or maybe had had scurried down like a mole.
But whatever had happened she wanted him back.

She got up and looked around, she went to his room
he was there in his bed, it was all a dream . . .
or should I say, a nightmare!

Jenny Hunt
Wrekin College, Telford

WATER PROBLEM

Drip, drop,
Went the water from the soap gurgling down the pipe.

Splish, splash,
The boy gave a big dash into the pool.

Pitter-patter,
Goes the rain on the drain, disappearing in a mysterious sewer.

Slip, slide,
The water has no grip in the river from the mountains.

And what's the problem?
The water flowing from the lakes.

Hessa Bouresli (12)
Wrekin College, Telford

WATER, WATER

Water, water, like a dream,
Softly flowing down a stream.
Water, water in the sea,
Making waves, how can that be?
Water, water in the river,
Fast flowing current makes me quiver.
Water, water let it flow
Through the tap, fast or slow.
Water, water, pitter-patter,
Falling through the sky.
Water, water,
Drip,
Drip,
Drip.

Joey Warnett (12)
Wrekin College, Telford

WATER AT HOME

We use water all the time
In our bath tubs, sinks and showers.
Using water isn't a crime,
We use water for hours and hours.

We have it in our drinks,
To cook our food.
We pour it down our sinks
You need to be in a very good mood.

Felicity Sharp (12)
Wrekin College, Telford

PRECIOUS WATER

The gush of water
The whoosh of a wave.
It just makes you think.
Is water the colour of blue ink?
1% is good.
The rest is really bad
Even if you've never had
A water fight or paddle.
That you wish you'd never had
Some say it makes you really mad.
Now say to yourself,
Water, water, water.
So next time
You have a water fight again
Or drink some water on an aeroplane,
Remember when you get to May
That it will rain another day.

Florian Sips (13)
Wrekin College, Telford

WATER

I give life to the grass
As I fall from the sky
Without me the birds
And the animals would die.

I give life to the rivers
The lakes and the sea
The fishes have homes
Just 'cause of me.

I give life to people
Who need me each day
They drink me and use me
At work and at play.

Can you imagine
A world without me?
No - it's impossible
So take care of me.

Vicky Hammond (12)
Wrekin College, Telford

AQUA

Water, water everywhere,
As blue as the sky in night air.
Powerful as a pride of lions,
In the moonlight it shines.

Clear as glass,
Gleaming in the sun.
Swimming and splashing,
Having good fun.

Like eating salt with your chips,
You can jump into it to have a quick dip.
The habitat of a small fish or large whale,
A play time for male or female.

Every drop is like a piece of gold,
Pure rainwater cannot be sold.
Water keeps us all alive,
Without it the human race would not survive.

Tom Hunter (12)
Wrekin College, Telford

I CAN

I can drip,
I can drop,
I can jump,
I can hop,
I can splish,
I can splosh.

When I boil,
I can pop,
When I'm left,
I just stop.

I cover 70% of this Earth,
That is what makes the surf.
I make 75% of your body
And my common name is water.

Ashley Smith (12)
Wrekin College, Telford

PLAYING IN THE WAVES

Playing in the waves,
With the salty taste,
Rather like tuna paste,
With water up my nose
And fishes at my toes.

Take a bodyboard
And a wave to shore.
In all the water pours.
Dive off the rocks,
The water's like building blocks.

Warren Harding (12)
Wrekin College, Telford

THE ELEPHANT

Grey, slow, thundering feet
yet so gentle,
gentle, giant, elegant mammal.
Crinkled skin,
folds of grey soft skin
fall around flapping ears
beating the heat with mud.
Flies buzz around, pushed away,
deep, thick mud, yet like paper
to an elephant.
Trunk tears through leaves
as though they were air.

But beware, for the elephant
can use his strength to his own ends.
thundering feet pound the earth
sending shocks so you know he's there,
sending animals large and small
running far away to safety.
Loud horn bellows issue from his trunk,
scaring even lions into hiding.
Eyes glare and flash,
ears bang against trees.

But the elephant is only angry for a reason,
man, an evil beast.
Powerful, peaceful and yet so defenceless
against, *bang, crack,*
death!

Cathy Drew (12)
Wrekin College, Telford

THE BUNNY NAMED BILL

There was a big, fat bunny
who liked eating honey.
But when it was sunny,
he preferred to suck a dummy.

His name, he said, was Bill
'I live by the mill;
can you see the hill?
It's where I have my fill.'

Then two more rabbits came
and one said, with disdain,
'Leave Bill alone! He's lame!'
'I think that he's insane!'

To which I replied, 'Mad?
He seems such a fine lad!
Surely he's not that bad
And look! You've made him sad!'

Then Bill spoke some more,
Saying, 'I feel like a door!
I would run to the moor,
But my legs are far too sore!'

So the other said,
'You see, he's wrong in the head!
We ask if he wants to be fed
And he tells us he's a bed!'

Now I know his case is dire,
I saw him hopping through the mire!
I was wrong to call the others liars,
But that's all from me now, by Master Matthew Humphreys Esquire.

Matthew Humphreys (13)
Wrekin College, Telford